Awakening
of the
DREAM RIDERS

GW00599484

LYNDA LOUISE MANGORO

To Sandy,
May the Dream Riders
bring a touch of
magic into your
life!
Love Lynda
x x

Mangoro

Published in 2011 by Juicy Living Publishing

www.JuicyLivingPublishing.com

Cover design by Lynda Mangoro

ISBN 978-0-9562546-2-7

Praise for this Book

What a fabulous book! Magical, clear and gripping, this is a story that any teenager, and indeed any adult, will certainly enjoy. Its essential message of love and the power of the imagination speaks to us all. A fascinating start to what I hope will be a long-running Dream Rider series.
– Anne Brooke, Author

This is a grand story in itself, rich in character, rich in their experiences of learning, growing, and being open to possibilities perhaps not considered before. Captivating, yet fun - whimsical, yet thought provoking. All in all a joyful look at a group of young people coming into their own maturity and...their precious 'gifts'
– Dee Moss, Energy Healing Facilitator

From the very first page I was taken in fully. I was pulled to know more. And I was not aware of the voyage I was about to embark upon as this wonderful child, Kyra, found the birthing of a gift that she had no idea was possible. I was pulled in at the soul level, for this work touches the soul with truth mingled into fiction. On the journey with Kyra, Liam, Noah, Crystal, Ray, and Marco I felt the full range of all of my emotions and the loss, the love, the life renewed in confirmation that each of these souls shared. I marvelled at the sync in which this book progressed and truly felt it more of a work of soul truth than fiction. This work touches at the soul level in a confirming way for those of us who have been made aware in this age. It will teach a great deal and resonate in the young souls soon to be awakened! Thank you for blessing my soul with this work.
– Laurie Hopkins, Author

This book is dedicated to my boys - thank you for sharing this journey with me and bringing wonder, inspiration, and plenty of smiles to me every single day. I love you endlessly.

Acknowledgements

In the writing of my first novel I've learned that bringing a book to life is truly a team effort. With that in mind, there are many people I wish to thank.

Michael, the Dream Riders wouldn't exist without you – we dreamed them up long before I wrote their first adventure on paper. Thank you for so often visiting my secret world with me. My boys, you inspire me every day with your inquisitive minds and open hearts. Dad, thank you for the rich lessons you taught me, they've flavoured many parts of this story and without them my passion for understanding life wouldn't be the same. Mum, Lorraine, Lorna, and Steven, I am blessed to be a part of such a wonderful, loving, supportive family, and I extend this acknowledgement to ALL my family and friends who make my life truly rich.

Lorraine you get an extra thank you. You've been a huge driving force behind the book and I wouldn't have finished it without you. Thank you for so much of your time, and your unfailing faith in the Dream Riders and in me.

Jodie, thank you for being my first test reader, and for your much needed words of encouragement. Dyan, thank you for helping me turn this book from a dream into a reality and taking my first tentative steps in the world of publishing. I truly appreciate you. Darryl, Jolene, Jean, Linda, and Katie – I cherish your friendship and your support – thank you.

Lilou, I thank you for the inspiration you provide by following your heart and living authentically. I thank you also for recognising and supporting my intention to reach many with my stories and for seeing the green light and making it happen. You are an angel in my life, for sure. Big leap – taken!

Much Love
Lynda

Chapter 1

Narrowly missing the lampshade hanging from the centre of the ceiling, Kyra dodged to the right with just a few inches to spare. She straightened herself up, attempting to gain control, but still moving too fast, unfamiliar with this new mode of travel. Her favourite unicorn poster suddenly loomed directly ahead. Pulling back, she slowed just in time to avoid a collision with the wall and sent herself tumbling backward through the air, rolling head over heels in a clumsy display of aero-gymnastics. Her shaggy cream carpet rushed up to meet her, closer with each spin. But there was no fear, only calmly suppressed excitement. Serenity took over, and with the next spin she pulled upward, the soft carpet tickling her bare toes as she swiftly ascended.

Phew, that was close! She circled the room again, this time in a more controlled manner, and then a third time, smoother still. Warm air embraced her as she glided gracefully, a golden beam of evening sunlight caressing her softly each time she drifted past the window. She was a bird. She was a shadow. She was free. Her heart swelled with glee as she thought of her family downstairs, unaware. Hovering above her bed she spun slowly in place, really mastering the movements now. Pointing her toes downward she stretched her arms up high and touched her fingers together like a ballerina. She wanted to laugh out loud but couldn't risk being heard. She felt she might burst with joy. She spun faster and faster and...suddenly a knock on her door, a loud voice. "Kyra?"

A jolt shook her body as she fell back onto her bed, her heart thudding. Sitting up quickly she panted, stunned to be grounded so suddenly, her head still flying around the room.

"Kyra?" her father called again through the door. "I'm making hot chocolate. Do you want some?"

"Yes, please, dad. I'll be down in a sec," she replied, hoping he wouldn't detect the strange note in her voice.

When she heard the tell-tale creaking of the bottom step as her father returned downstairs, she collapsed backward on the bed. That was unbelievable she thought, and pulled the pillow from beneath her head, hugging it close to her and laughing into it softly. I can fly. It sounded surreal. It sounded impossible. She could barely comprehend it.

It was the most amazing thing that had ever happened to Kyra Sutton, and that was saying something. It was, quite literally, a dream come true. It was a persistent but blissful dream of soaring lazily over endless fields of golden corn, the sun warming her back and melting her worries, a gentle breeze sweeping through her hair. Now it was happening for real.

Okay, so in reality she flew with far less grace than in her dreams. But the exhilaration that had flooded through her as she'd swooped across her bedroom was like nothing she'd experienced before, nonetheless. It was a trillion times better than a rollercoaster. She wanted to do it again, to experience that awesome sensation. She wanted to open her window and take off into the evening sky. She wanted to live her dream.

"Kyra?" her father's voice boomed up the stairs again. "Hot chocolate's ready."

"Coming," she called, and sighed.

Flying would have to wait.

Chapter 2

Mornings in the Sutton household were always hectic. Well, for Kyra at least. She seemed to have inherited the position of combined mother and maid by default. Nobody ever actually asked her to do anything, but her father didn't have a clue about anything domestic and her brother seemed to live on another planet most of the time. So she wasn't left with much choice. Either she took on the role or they all lived in complete chaos, and probably starved to death.

They'd survived almost exclusively on beans on toast for the first six months without her mum, until Kyra had started downloading recipes for her dad to follow. Even then she'd had to do most of it for him. He'd had no idea how to even boil an egg. Although funny at first, the kitchen disasters had very quickly lost their comic value.

The days of having to worry about nothing more than getting herself ready for school in the morning were long gone. This morning she'd already showered and dressed, prepared their lunches, tidied the lounge and kitchen, and packed her school bag, all before eating breakfast. Alone. Lone breakfasts were also pretty standard these days, but today she was grateful for that. It would have been difficult to concentrate on the standard day to day chitchat when all she wanted to do was shout from the rafters, "I CAN FLY!"

Today she was buzzing with a new alertness, and all her senses were heightened, as if she'd awakened some dormant part of herself. Easy sleep and shapeless dreams had been invaded by the sound of frogs croaking in the small garden pond. She could hear them as loudly as if she'd been sitting right beside them, and she'd awoken to the unmistakable smell of the rosemary bush in the front garden. When she concentrated she'd been able to identify at least three other plants by their scent too. It was incredible. She felt more alive, more aware of every little thing, and she knew it had something to do with the flying. It had changed her somehow.

Eager to share her news with her best friend Lauren, she'd been clock-watching the whole morning, willing the little hands to move faster. She'd showered and dressed in record time, although she could never be bothered to do much more than run a brush through her curly mop of mahogany hair. Makeup was just a pointless hassle in her opinion, and luckily for her, her large green eyes were framed with naturally thick lashes. Clothes were just as easy. Every morning she just slung on the first thing that caught her eye in the wardrobe. All that remained before she could leave was to make sure her dad got to work on time. "Dad, are you awake?" she called, knocking on his bedroom door. "You only have twenty minutes 'til you need to leave."

The door opened with a creak, and her father emerged looking like a grizzly bear with a sore head. Well, a very scrawny grizzly bear. His eyes were underlined by dark smudges, his face covered in stubble. He looked like he'd been on an all night drinking session. But Kyra knew him better than that. It was more likely to have been an all night computer programming session. During the last year he seemed to have become even more of a geek than he'd been previously, which she wouldn't have believed possible if she hadn't seen it with her own eyes. At least he's dressed already she thought, rolling her eyes with a smile and handing him a mug of coffee.

"Your porridge is in the microwave, sandwiches in the kitchen by the kettle."

"You're a gem. Have I ever told you that?" he asked, and pecked her on the cheek as he passed her, heading down the stairs.

"Only every morning, dad, and by the way, that tie doesn't match that shirt," she told his retreating back.

She didn't bother even attempting to wake Liam on her way out. He probably wouldn't surface until at least lunch time. Trotting down the stairs two at a time, she slung her backpack over her shoulder and shouted "bye" to anyone who could hear.

Chapter 3

Ignoring the slightly sour taste of milk that had just crept past its use-by date, Noah Pinkerton ate his soggy cornflakes mechanically, his mind elsewhere. It was almost seven A.M. and that little voice in his head told him he should start getting his packed lunch ready and wash his breakfast dishes, but his mind was failing to connect with his body. Shattered from another night of broken sleep, he stayed at the table, spoon in hand, long after his bowl was empty.

Noah was used to the stillness of the house and knew its every creaky floorboard, every noisy pipe and draughty window. Long ago he'd drawn up a mental floor plan and knew how to avoid setting off these noises during the long lonely nights, feeling protected only when cloaked in complete silence. Every slight noise twanged his tightly wound nerves, each sound indicating a possible threat.

The distant bark of a dog jerked him from his reverie and he dragged himself up from the table, carrying his dish to the sink. This has to stop one day, he thought, as he rinsed his bowl and spoon. A knock at the front door caused his heart to gallop, and his hands froze under the tepid tap water. With perspiration forming on his brow, he held his breath, as if pausing in time would make them go away.

Being a man of science, and proud of his logical approach to life, Noah wouldn't admit that he could be a victim of irrational fears.

He was stronger than that. Still he didn't move. Another knock at the door travelled through the hallway, through his ear canal and into his brain, setting off a pang of irritation – irritation at himself for allowing fear to control him. He wouldn't be that person. He wouldn't be a coward. And not being a coward meant opening the door and facing his tormentor.

Depositing the bowl on the draining board and shutting off the tap, he stepped into the dimness of the downstairs hallway and slowly moved toward the front door.

The sound of a key turning in the lock sent a flood of relief through him. It was just his mum returning from her night shift at the hospital. Slumping against the wall, suppressed adrenaline rushed into his veins and weakened him, his shaky legs threatening to collapse beneath him. The door opened to reveal his mother, still dressed in her pale blue nurse uniform and struggling to carry three bursting Co-op bags. She let out a little squeal of fright at the sight of him. "I thought you'd left already. You didn't answer the door. Took me ages to get to my key with all this stuff. So are you gonna help me then, or just stand there like a sack of potatoes?"

"Sorry mum, I was upstairs when you knocked," he lied. Springing into action, he relieved her of the bags, carrying them through to the kitchen.

"Good night?" he enquired, as he always did. He knew her work was long and tiring, although she never complained.

"Not bad," she answered, beginning to unpack the shopping. "Pretty quiet actually. And yours?"

"Same. Did my homework, went next door for a while to work on the website. Came home, watched some telly, and then went to bed." A brief summary, it didn't include the nasty text message he'd received, or the countless times he'd crept down in the night to ensure the door really was locked, and that he really was alone. He ran his hand through his thick shaggy black mop to conceal his guilty expression.

They had the same conversation every time she returned home, a habit they'd picked up years ago when Noah was six and his mum had first returned to work. As if sharing all the boring details of their separate lives would somehow create a bridge between them, a lifeline to cling to that would stop them from drifting too far apart.

"Are you sure you're okay? You look tired. Anything you want to talk about?" she enquired. Not purely a mother's intuition, the dark smears under his eyes and his pallid complexion gave away his lack of sleep.

"No, honest mum, I'm fine. Some dog down the street kept making a racket, that's all." Not a complete lie, just a little twist of the truth. She eyed him suspiciously.

"Honey, I can stop taking all these night shifts if you'd prefer. I can go back to doing days."

He would love nothing more, but wouldn't admit that to her in a million years. Since changing to night shifts a few months earlier her wages had almost doubled, lifting a huge pressure from her, giving her enough money to make ends meet and even squeeze in a few little treats for them now and again, like KFC on the weekends, and a pair of Nikes for him when it wasn't even his birthday.

He could see how much she enjoyed being able to go to bingo once a month, and to pay for his school trips without suffering the embarrassment of having to explain to the head teacher that she couldn't afford it. And now she could sleep during the day while he was at school. She was always awake and fresh when he returned home, always able to prepare a meal for them to eat together before she left for work, something they hadn't been able to do for years. So no, he wouldn't ruin all that just because of his own childish fears of being alone at night.

"Don't be silly, mum. It's fine." He waved a hand dismissively. "Listen, you go lie down, I'll finish unpacking this lot."

"Thanks, Noah. You're a good boy," she said with a tired smile, and rubbed his shoulder before disappearing upstairs to sleep.

He'd finished putting all the shopping away, made his lunch, and was just making sure he'd got all the books he needed for the day ahead when the second knock at the front door came. His heart sank. He'd allowed himself to believe they wouldn't come today after all. This time he knew immediately it was trouble.

Hoping his mum was asleep already and hadn't been disturbed by the noise, he went to the door quickly to avoid a further knock. The rules were different now his mum was home. He simply had to be strong. There was no room for childishness.

Marco DiCarmello was smiling smugly at the other side of the door, with a mate lingering just behind him exactly as Noah had expected. There was always a mate, usually a different one each time, providing Marco with a fresh audience to show off to. The mate always fit perfectly into the same generic template, as if there was a factory somewhere churning them out, The Wannabe Bully Factory. They were always shorter than Marco in order to boost his self-image, always scrawnier too, but with an edge about them that suggested they had a mean streak. They always had their school shirt un-tucked, and their tie either missing or hanging loosely in defiance of conforming to the acceptable. It was so predictable it was almost funny. Noah was gripped by a sudden urge to laugh despite the dread in his gut, but he valued his teeth far too much.

"Alright Pinky? I've come for my coursework," Marco stated. His wide legged stance and his crossed arms were just as predictable and threatening as everything else about the scene. Taller and stockier than the average fourteen year old boy, his olive skin was marred by a scattering of red acne, his black hair cropped short. He'd cornered Noah the previous day and ordered him to draw up a plan for his history coursework. The demand had been reiterated in a text message during the night, along with a very clear explanation of what would happen if he failed to comply.

"I told you before, I'm not doing it," Noah replied, looking into the larger boy's emotionless green eyes, his voice firm but low, desperate not to wake his mum. He had no doubt that if she came downstairs, Marco would put on a good act, turn on the charm, and probably pretend to be a friend calling for him. But still, he didn't want to risk her finding out what was going on. And besides she really needed her rest and he didn't want her to be disturbed.

Noah couldn't see a way out, couldn't see an end, yet still he wouldn't endure the humiliation of giving Marco what he wanted, even though he knew it was this defiance that made him the bully's favourite target.

He knew what was coming. He'd never once given in to Marco; never done his homework for him, never given him money, or cried like a baby when he was told to. He'd never followed Marco's orders and he never would. They both knew that Marco no longer expected him to. The coursework was simply the latest excuse to use in front of his generic wannabe-bully friend, justification for lashing out at somebody smaller than he, somebody who wouldn't fight back.

Noah tensed his stomach muscles in anticipation of the first blow, but it struck him in the chest this time and sent him flying backward, his back thudding onto the hallway carpet, the air bursting from his lungs. Winded and in immense pain, he wanted to cry out, but wouldn't give his attackers the pleasure. And still through the agony, he was terrified his mum would be disturbed. He couldn't bear the thought of her finding him like this, of causing her more problems. By simply existing he'd caused her enough pain to last a lifetime.

He couldn't have cried out even if he'd wanted to. He was unable to even breathe. Gasping uselessly for air, his lungs deflated balloons, he felt like a fish out of water, desperate for oxygen. Finally air came, just as he thought he might pass out, and he managed to pull himself to a sitting position, lacking the energy required to stand. He glared at Marco, summoning all the bravado he could muster, cautiously aware that his face was at perfect kicking height, preparing to dodge Marco's clumpy boot if necessary.

"I warned you, didn't I? You can't say I didn't warn you," Marco growled, his eyes glowing with menacing amusement. "You got all those brains in there; you really ought to share 'em. Too selfish, that's your problem." He gave a wry smile, and glanced back at his supporting onlooker, seeking appreciation of his crass humour. Wannabe-bully was squirming in the background, looking around

16

shiftily, afraid they might get caught. He managed a fake smile for his hero.

Marco turned back to Noah. "I'll 'ave to sort you out after school matey, I'm a busy man. Don't worry, I know exactly where to find you, don't I?" He spat for dramatic effect. And although Noah's stomach curled up with disgust as the spit dripped down his cheek. He didn't move to wipe it away, but simply held eye contact with his tormentor. Wannabe-bully spat too, the closest he'd dared come to actually participating in the attack. His saliva landed ineffectively next to Noah's foot, giving Noah at least a small sense of victory.

As the boys walked down the path and away down the street without a backward glance, Noah allowed himself to drink in heavy lungfuls of air and moaned quietly, the raw pain in his chest sending waves of nausea through him. He wondered if there was a broken rib, but knew he wouldn't get it checked out unless absolutely necessary. It would lead to too many questions. Pulling himself slowly to his feet, he smiled despite the pain. He was proud he hadn't given in. It was about the best outcome he could hope for anymore.

He was also grateful they hadn't thrown eggs this time. At least he wouldn't have to buy more Vanish for the hallway carpet.

Chapter 4

Spring was marching speedily toward what promised to be a scorching summer, and as Kyra trotted down her front path, her bubbly mood was heightened by the unbroken blue sky and the warmth of the sun, already beating down with determination. Pausing on the pavement, she spun in a slow circle, absorbing the spectrum of colours that surrounded her, breathing them in, feeling them feed her in a way she'd never experienced before. She turned to close the front gate behind her just as Noah emerged from next door.

"Hi Noah!" she called, and wandered the few steps to his gate. They'd been next door neighbours forever. Well, since before they were both born, at least. Kyra's parents had lived on Saffron Road since they were first married back in 1990, and Noah's mum had moved there when she was expecting him. Their mothers had formed a companionship based on nothing deeper than coinciding pregnancies and babies born just three days apart. Beyond that they'd had little in common. The babies, however, had grown to be firm friends.

"Hey, Ky," Noah replied far too brightly, his smile forced. She immediately detected the flatness in his voice, and as he walked slowly down the path, she also noticed the slump in his shoulders. She'd bet anything Marco was hassling him again.

An uneasy knot formed in her gut. Noah was such a sweet person. He didn't deserve to be the target of a nasty piece of work like Marco DiCarmello.

"So what did he do this time?" she asked, knowing he'd dismiss it.

"Nothing serious," he answered, predictably, fiddling with a zip on his bag. It was no surprise he didn't try to deny it completely. He knew she'd see straight through him.

"Are you okay?" she asked, concerned.

"I'm fine" he smiled, still only making brief eye contact.

"I'm telling you, Noah, you should speak to your mum about it. You can't let him keep doing this to you," Kyra said gently, knowing she was fighting a losing battle but not sure what else she could do short of having a word with Marco herself. She knew Noah wouldn't thank her for that.

When he'd originally confessed to his mum about the bullying, way back when it had started in year seven, she'd immediately moved him to another school despite his protests, terrified that something awful would happen to him. He'd since confided to Kyra that Marco had continued to hassle him outside of school hours, but as far as his mum was concerned the bullying had stopped the minute he changed schools. And he wanted to keep it that way.

"And I'm telling you it's nothing serious," he replied firmly.

She raised her eyebrows but didn't pursue it. There was no point. They'd had this conversation a million times and they both knew he wouldn't tell, yet neither could think of any alternative solutions. He reckoned he could put up with it until Marco "grew out of it" insisting it was only a few harmless text messages and prank calls. She suspected there was more he wasn't telling her but respected his desire to not discuss it.

Trying to think of a quick subject change, she wished she could share the one mammoth thing that was occupying her mind, but she couldn't. Noah was the last person she wanted to know about her new-found super powers. It might seem strange that she would keep such a humongous secret from her closest and oldest friend, but that was the exact reason why she had to keep him in the dark. She didn't want to risk their friendship.

Noah was the most analytical person she knew, and also one of the cleverest. She was sure he'd think she'd gone loopy, dismiss her experiences as hallucinations, or worse, pure fantasy. He was the kind of person who needed a scientific formula before even entertaining the possibility of believing something out of the ordinary, and the thought of losing her best friend had always prevented her from confiding in him – although there'd been many times when she'd come close.

"So how's the website going?" she asked, a sudden burst of inspiration reminding her of the best subject to both distract him and cheer him up. It worked. His face brightened visibly.

"Not bad, actually. Monkey hit a thousand last night," he said with a large hint of pride in his voice. Most people would have more luck reading hieroglyphics than deciphering any meaning from that sentence, but Kyra had been exposed to geek-speak for so long, she understood immediately. Monkey referred to "Monkey Cove," the website Noah had been building for the last six months, and the number one thousand was the latest member count.

Noah wasn't building the website alone. He was working in partnership with Kyra's father. A fully fledged "code monkey," Norman Sutton worked part time on programming contracts, and spent every other minute of his life trying to design the next big thing, the invention that would change their lives. Robots, gadgets, tools, Kyra had lost count of the "big things" that had thus far failed to change their weekly food budget, let alone their lives.

Mr. Sutton had been delighted when a few months previously Noah had started showing an interest in creating websites, as it was the next area he'd already decided to explore. The pair now spent hours each week developing Monkey Cove, an online community they described as a "Knowledge Sharing Portal for Programmers." She secretly referred to it as "Facebook for Geeks."

"That's fantastic news, Noah. Congratulations!" she gushed, genuinely happy for him, despite the fact that anything remotely technical bored her to tears. She was bursting to share her own news with someone. She had to see Lauren.

"Noah, I've got to get going or I'll be late. I'll probably see you later though."

"You've got ages 'til you need to be at school. How come you're out so early anyway?" Noah asked. His own school was on the other side of town, and he usually left at least half an hour before she did.

"Oh, I just have to see Lauren, nothing important." With a wave she rushed down the road before he could ask any further questions.

"Yeah okay, see you later," he called after her with an amused shake of his head.

Chapter 5

It was as if she'd stepped into a fairy-tale overnight. This flying business had definitely changed her somehow. Everything around her was transformed from average to radiant. It was strange and surreal, but in a good way. Blossoms decorated the trees along her way, coloured from a palette of soft pastels, and a chorus of morning birds serenaded her as she strolled to Lauren's house just a few streets from her own. A few streets in distance, that is, but a million miles away in every other respect. Their streets were separated by the railway line which marked a very definitive divide in areas. Kyra lived just north of the tracks and Lauren lived just south.

Lauren's family home was large, white, and detached. It always reminded Kyra of a Spanish villa like those she'd seen on holiday programs. It stood proudly on a wide oak lined avenue which stretched lazily down to the beach. Even on a normal day walking down this street was like stepping into another world somewhere exotic and far away, a feeling enhanced by the palm trees that adorned many of the spacious front gardens. The inside of Lauren's house was even more breath-taking than outside. Each and every room looked like a spread in a glossy magazine. It was a world apart from Kyra's own family home, a run of the mill three bedroom terraced house on a narrow street whose gardens were more likely to boast broken car parts and old mattresses than palm trees.

She turned the corner and could see Lauren sitting on the stone wall that edged her front garden, her head tilted up toward the sun and her eyes closed, soaking up the warm rays. Her golden hair spilled softly behind her, capturing the sunlight like a scene in a shampoo advert. Lauren wanted to be an actress one day. She certainly looked the part, and had the confidence for it too.

"Spill, Miss Sutton. Tell all," Lauren ordered, without moving or even opening her eyes as Kyra approached. "What's so important that you wake me up at six in the morning with a text demanding I get up and leave early?"

Kyra stood directly in front of Lauren and stared at her friend's closed eyelids, suppressing a smile. "I can fly," she said simply and smiled when Lauren's pale blue eyes shot open.

"You what?" Lauren asked, though she'd heard perfectly well. "Is this a joke?"

A reasonable question, Kyra thought.

"Nope, it's no joke. Really. Truly. I can fly."

Lauren jumped up, grabbing her schoolbag from the ground beside her.

"Come on," she said, taking Kyra's elbow and steering her toward the street. "Let's walk and talk. Tell me everything." Kyra smiled and allowed herself to be pulled along by her best friend. Lauren's willingness to accept anything as a possibility was one of the many things Kyra loved about her, and it was their biggest bond.

In many ways the girls couldn't be more different. Lauren was confident, outspoken, and pretty. In contrast Kyra was shy and quiet and, in her opinion, distinctly average in the looks department. And while she was no Einstein, she liked to keep up to date with world news and her interests extended way beyond boys and makeup.

Fate, in the form of their geography teacher, had thrown the two girls together on Lauren's first day at the school in year eight, about a year and a half previously, when the class had been instructed to choose partners for an upcoming project. Most of their classmates had paired off immediately, leaving Lauren, who'd just moved to the area and didn't know anyone, and Kyra, who had no real friends in the school since Noah had transferred.

Kyra had never been particularly interested in making friends, especially with girls. Refusing to be a sheep and follow the latest fashions or music trends or whatever, she knew she was seen as a bit of an oddball. And it suited her just fine that girls in school steered clear of her. She preferred her own company anyway. And so she was surprised to find herself completely relaxed in Lauren's company. She actually really liked her, despite the fact she acted like such a girl.

Initially it had been her honesty that had attracted Kyra. She said what was on her mind and she said it without mentally editing first. The first words Lauren had said to her were: "Oh my God, look at you. You're so cute and diddy, like a pixie! You are gorgeous! I don't know why you're so determined to hide it. Your eyes are amazing, like a cat's, and you're lucky your hair is so thick and shiny naturally, 'cause I bet you don't use serum right? And your lips, look at them, so plump and lovely. Angelina, eat your heart out. We need to get you some cherry lip gloss."

Kyra had just stared open-mouthed at this human whirlwind, not knowing what to think, but immediately respecting the girl for speaking her mind. Lauren never stopped talking. She talked for hours about everything and anything. She embraced every subject with energy and enthusiasm, and Kyra, usually private and withdrawn, had found herself nattering back as if it were contagious.

Kyra had soon discovered her first impressions of the new girl were way off the mark. Over the next few weeks she'd found Lauren's personality to sparkle as much as her hair and makeup. Despite her looks and money, Lauren didn't have a superior attitude or look down on others, as Kyra had expected. She'd also been an eager partner for their geography project, disproving Kyra's assumption that she was an airhead.

It wasn't many weeks before that Kyra had revealed her biggest secret to Lauren, one day during a game of truth or dare. It was a secret that she'd sworn at the age of five she would never share with another living soul. Her parents had accused her of making it up. They hadn't believed a word she'd said. Lauren had believed her immediately. Kyra had studied her friend's face as she had divulged her story and hadn't seen even the smallest flicker of doubt. In fact, Lauren's awestruck reaction had actually made Kyra feel special, and gifted, like maybe she should be proud of her secret instead of feeling like a weirdo as she always had.

The pair had soon become inseparable and had remained that way ever since. Kyra was worried that her friend might actually pee herself with excitement about this new discovery as she skipped along hurriedly dragging Kyra with her. "Lauren, slow down. And let go, you're hurting my arm," Kyra said with a laugh. Lauren loosened her grip but didn't let go completely, hooking her arm through Kyra's, looking at her expectantly as they walked, her neatly plucked eyebrows raised in a silent prompt.

"Ok," Kyra started. "It happened last night after dinner. I was just lying on the bed chilling, and suddenly I felt all funny, kind of weird. I don't know how to explain it. My body went kind of shaky all over, like, buzzing, and before I knew it I was rising up off the bed, just kind of floating. I kept going up until the ceiling was just inches in front of my face, and then I suddenly thought maybe I would hit it. So I stared floating sideways instead."

"Oh My God, weren't you scared? What happened next? I mean, how, you know, just how?" Lauren blurted, her eyes wide with amazement, and then bit her bottom lip in an effort to stop herself from interrupting further. She sank down onto a wooden bench, finding it difficult to concentrate on Kyra's story and walk at the same time. Kyra sat next to her.

"No, that's the strangest thing. You'd think I would be scared, right? I mean it's not every day you find out that you can fly. But at the time I just felt completely calm, like it was the most natural thing in the world. It was only afterward I felt a little freaked out, but only because dad knocked on the door. I thought he was going to just walk in on me. I mean, just imagine."

Lauren pulled a face that indicated she could quite clearly imagine the scenario.

"Anyway, after supper I really wanted to try again. I wanted to fly outside instead of just in my room. But I didn't dare do it with dad and Liam in the house. And then I remembered that stupid math homework, and I was knackered by the time I'd finished that. I fell asleep watching telly."

Kyra was talking faster and faster, her excitement growing all the more as she recalled the experience. The urge to do it again was pulling her like a magnet. For a fleeting moment she considered skipping school and returning home, but it would be pointless. Liam would be there and she wouldn't be able to relax.

"Oh My God," Lauren said again, evidently having lost the ability to extract a different phrase from her vocabulary. "Okay, I don't get how you did it? I mean, did you like sprout wings out of your back or something, or is it like teleken-whatever-its-called, where you move objects with the power of your thoughts but you moved yourself instead?"

"Well that's the weirdest part. It didn't even occur to me to wonder how it was happening at the time. I just kind of accepted it. So after floating across the room I kind of swooped around in a semi-circle so I was facing back the way I'd come and I glanced down toward the bed and... "

"Well, hello, girls, fancy seeing you here."

They both looked up, startled, to see Luke Higgins, a wispy blonde boy who considered himself to be the Romeo of year nine, smiling down at them. Unfortunately for him, nobody else shared his opinion of himself, and he was often the victim of ridicule and sniggering behind his back. Lauren, unfailingly nice to everyone, particularly underdogs and the downtrodden, had made the mistake of being pleasant to Luke a few months ago and had earned his undying affection in return.

"Hey, Luke," Lauren said while Kyra smiled politely, annoyed at the interruption. "We were actually just in the middle of a private conversation."

His metal adorned smile widened. "Aha, and I bet I can guess exactly who you were talking about, hey, Lauren." He winked. Kyra was reminded of the animated cheese string from the advert, he was all long and pale, and kinda gangly. Seriously. Kyra thought if she pulled his arm it would just keep on stretching like rubber. She stifled a laugh.

"Yes very funny, Luke. We'll catch you later, ok?" Lauren turned back to Kyra pointedly, but Luke was either not getting the hint or completely ignoring it. Kyra was itching to tell him to get lost, but kept her mouth shut.

"It's after eight already. You'll be late if you sit around gossiping about me for much longer. Come on, why don't you lovely ladies let me escort you to school?"

Kyra bit the inside of her cheek to prevent a sarcastic remark from escaping, trying to follow Lauren's example and be nice, grateful that at least he hadn't made any vulgar remarks about meeting for a drool-swapping session behind the bike sheds this time, as had been his cringe inducing suggestion last week. A glance at her phone told her he was right. They needed to get going and it was clear he wasn't planning on leaving them alone.

In silent agreement the girls stood and walked the rest of the way with Luke, much to his delight. They gratefully parted company from him at the large black iron gates of the school. Students were filling the playground, reluctantly sauntering toward the entrance, and Kyra whispered a promise to Lauren that she would finish her story as soon as they found an opportunity to be alone. Entering the building, they were swept along in a blue and white tide of uniforms.

Chapter 6

Should a truant officer happen to wander past the Hill Road parade of shops whilst patrolling the streets of Cranley, he would certainly net himself a decent haul, especially if it was that time of day when school was due to let out. Just around the corner from the Cranley High, it was a perfect position from which students wagging from school could show off to the other kids as they left. Two back to back wooden benches and a phone box, littered and heavily decorated with graffiti, provided all the comforts needed by kids with nothing better to do than hang out until the clock struck the hour when they could return home without raising parents' suspicions.

Marco had been to school that morning, but had left for an important doctor's appointment after lunch. He had to see the doctor quite regularly these days, at least twice a week, in fact, according to the note from his dad. Any other person would be seriously worried about their health, but as Marco had actually written the notes himself, he knew there was no cause for concern.

They were quite productive, all these doctor appointments, allowing him to nip into town for a while, where he usually wandered round the shops, nicked some stuff, sweets, magazines, sometimes even CDs. Not that he really wanted or needed any of that stuff. He simply did it for the thrill and for bragging rights. Whatever he got up to during these afternoons of freedom, he always made sure he was back at the Hill Road parade at least half an hour before the bell rang.

By that time there were usually at least fifteen kids messing around outside the shops, some from different year groups, all of whom should have been in school. It was the time of day Marco relished because of the opportunities it may present to him – opportunities to show off to the older, more rebellious kids. Everything he did was designed to make them see how cool he was, to get their respect. Marco thrived on the reactions he gained from others. Be it admiration, amusement, or fear, Marco saw it as respect. It gave him self-worth, although he knew his desire for respect made him dangerous.

There were a few occasions when he scared himself with the lengths he was willing to go just to impress the right people. And one of those occasions came along a few minutes after the bell rang to indicate the end of the school day.

"Alright, mate? Can I have a pack of ten?" a skinny blonde boy asked, looking down toward Marco's feet instead of into his eyes. Anyone who knew Marco knew better than to do anything that might antagonize him, even look at him in the wrong way.

Aaron Stillman was in year eight, although he was so small he looked more like he belonged in primary school. The pale brown freckles marching across his nose didn't do anything to make him look any closer to his real age. There was no way in hell he would get served cigarettes, which was why he was one of Marco's regular customers. Fishing a box out of his tatty backpack, Marco handed it over, but only after the kid gave up nearly double the retail value of the pack.

Looking older than his fourteen years, mostly due to his large build, definitely had many benefits for Marco. One of the biggest was finding it easy to get served, and Marco spent at least one evening a week visiting news agents all over town to stockpile fags, always dragging along a couple of members of his fan club so he had an audience when he emerged successfully from each shop waving his treasure.

The cigarettes were another means to gain respect. He personally found the habit repugnant and would rather drink toilet water than consider smoking. But when he'd noticed how many kids at school smoked, he'd devised his plan and it worked like a gem. He bought the cheapest cigarettes available and sold them to younger kids at a large profit, gaining their respect while endearing himself to the older kids by giving the impression he cared more about making money than picking up habits. If anyone ever questioned why he didn't smoke, he could simply answer that he would have to be stupid to smoke his profits – he might as well roll up a twenty pound note and smoke that. Not that anyone would ask again. The black eye and bloody nose he'd given the last person who questioned him had seen to that.

"Cheers," Aaron muttered and turned back toward his friends who were loitering nervously a few feet away.

"Wait a minute Stillman. Why the rush? You not got time for a chat with your old mate?" Marco called, enjoying the mixed emotions he saw flash across the boy's face as he turned back to him, a flicker of hope and a large dose of panic. He could guess what the kid was thinking: Is my luck in? Am I finally gonna get to be Marco's mate and hang out with him? Or am in deep shit?

"Yeah, course I have, mate," Aaron replied, trying to look like he wasn't bricking it. His mates in the background were now fidgeting, sensing trouble. It was obvious they wanted to be anywhere else but there at that moment in time, but couldn't lose face or let down a mate.

"Well, that's good." Marco jumped down from the back of the bench where he'd been sitting like a king on his throne, and draped an arm around Aaron's back, emphasizing the size difference between them to ensure he'd get a straight answer. "Because somebody grassed up my little business to Mr. Duffy and I wanna know who."

"It wasn't me, mate. I wouldn't do that. I promise."

Marco laughed an unnecessarily loud laugh designed to draw

attention, feeling himself building up for a show.

"Well I know it wasn't you, Stillman. That would just be really dumb wouldn't it? You'd be losing your only source then." He hit the boy playfully round the head, hard enough to hurt just a little bit. Aaron was clever enough to not show any reaction at all.

"But you're Mr. Popular in year eight, right? And it's bound to be a sniveling year eight pussy who did it. You got ears all over the place. You must know something?" Marco was looking at him accusingly now.

"I haven't heard anything about it, honest I haven't. I'd tell you if I had." Aaron's voice had taken on a pleading quality, although he suspected it didn't matter what he said. Marco was obviously gearing up for a scrap and he was in the firing line.

He was saved when another gaggle of year eight kids passing by on their way home caught Marco's attention, and one of them – the biggest nerd in the year – made the mistake of making eye contact.

"What you looking at? I bet it was you, weren't it? You grassed me up!" Marco knew it was a ridiculous accusation, but he had a crowd to play up to now and a role to fill.

"I don't know what you're talking about. I don't even know who you are," the kid replied and started walking even faster, giving Marco just the ammunition he needed.

"What the hell do you think you're doing you little piece of...did you just turn your back on me when I was talking to you? Ain't you got no respect at all?" Marco had reached the group by this point and grabbed the kid by the back of his collar, making sure he got some hair and skin in his grip too.

"No, I didn't mean to. Sorry, I... "

But he was cut off when Marco poked him hard in the chest.

"It was you, weren't it? You dobbed me in – that's why you're trying to run away from me." He poked the terrified boy over and over again, forcing him to walk backward with every push. "Yeah, I know it was you. I don't know your name, but I know it was you. You've got it in for me. Think you're smart, don't you? Don't try lying to me, son. I've got you now."

Almost all the kids outside the shops were watching now, their eyes glued to the scene with a mix of horror and excitement. Marco knew his accusations were unreasonable, he also knew the crowd's anticipation could push him over the edge but the amount of respect he could gain was seductive, spurring him on.

The volume of the murmuring crowd grew. "Leave it, Marco, he's only a kid," called one passing girl.

"He ain't no kid. He stitched me up, you stupid cow!" Marco responded and lifted his right foot behind him, then swung it hard toward the boy's shins in a scythe motion, sweeping his legs from under him and causing him to crash to the pavement. Marco registered gasps from the crowd, and buoyed from all the attention, he moved to strike the boy again as he lay on the ground. But he stopped at the last minute. The kid was crying uncontrollably and Marco's audience was starting to look a little agitated, even concerned.

Realising that more violence wouldn't be popular with the crowd, he moved in close and shouted in the kid's face instead. The boy barely heard him over his own racking sobs, snot, and dribble bubbling from his nose and mouth. Curled up in a ball on the pavement with his eyes tightly shut, he was wishing Marco away, like he used to wish away the boogey man in his wardrobe.

Marco would have carried on had the boy's reaction been tougher, but he could feel himself losing his audience. The stupid kid had messed things up. What a baby. Marco wished he'd picked on somebody a bit bigger, somebody who might have fought back, although not someone his own size, of course.

"Go on, get out of here, you've been warned now," he told the kid, retreating slowly. But the kid didn't move, or even open his eyes.

"I said push off while you've still got the chance!"

This was turning into an embarrassment. He had to regain control of the show. Grabbing him by the collar Marco hoisted up his subject, who looked up tentatively once on his feet, shaking visibly.

"You better run before I change my mind," Marco growled.

Somehow, despite legs of jelly, the boy ran until he was out of sight, his friends following behind him.

Chapter 7

The day appeared to be conspiring against them - Kyra had found no opportunity to talk to Lauren in private and finish telling her story. Distracted all day, she'd been unable to concentrate on anything. History was a blur, and Science had passed in one long daydream. Time had crept along like an uphill tortoise and every class was more tedious than the last. Kyra was nearly tearing her hair out by the time the final bell rang.

"Come on, let's go to my place," she instructed Lauren, linking arms with her friend as they flooded out of school with the rest of the crowd. Her brother's habits were somewhat erratic, but he was rarely home at this time of day and her father would get back at half five on the dot giving them a couple of hours alone. They strode resolutely through the open gates, heads down, avoiding interruptions.

No such luck.

A black convertible Beamer pulled up alongside them, and the dark tinted window slid down to reveal an older and even more beautiful version of Lauren.

"Hi, Mrs. Lockett," Kyra said, her heart sinking, guessing immediately what was coming. She was going to lose her chance to finish telling her story. Again.

"Hi there, Kyra," Lauren's mother replied with a smile, before turning her attention to her daughter. "Honey, I'm so sorry, but something's come up with the Carlson case and I have to go back to the office for a couple of hours. I need you to come home and watch Lily for a while."

Kyra glanced into the back of the car and smiled at Lauren's little sister. A cute little mini-me of her older sibling, Lila had the same wide blue eyes and silky pale blonde hair as Lauren, and looked adorable sucking her thumb and cuddling her Iggle Piggle toy. Honestly, you couldn't make it up - the three Lockett females were like clones of each other. It was extraordinary.

"Muu-uum," Lauren sing-songed in protest. "I was going to Kyra's. We have some work to do." Her voice trailed off, defeated, realising there was no point in arguing.

Her mother was a solicitor, but only worked part time so she could be with Lily. On the occasions she was required outside her normal hours, like today, Lauren had to step in as babysitter.

"I'm so sorry, honey, I can't do anything about it. Kyra's welcome to come back too, and you can do your work at our house. I left a lasagne in the oven. It just needs to be heated up, and there's ginger cake too."

Mrs. Lockett was like some kind of domestic goddess, as well as a successful career woman. Sometimes Kyra wondered if their family had moved here from another planet, one occupied by a race of people who were perfect in every way.

"Thanks, Mrs. L., but I need to get home so I can put the dinner on." Although hugely tempted, Kyra couldn't miss this small window of time to fly. It was becoming like a physical need now. She had to get home – with or without Lauren.

"I understand, honey," Mrs Lockett said. Kyra detected a note of pity in her voice. She knew it well. She'd heard that same tone numerous times since her mum had gone.

"I really am sorry Lauren can't come today. I can drop you at home if you'd like?" Lauren's mum asked with a smile. Kyra accepted the offer, eager to get home as quickly as possible. She clambered into the back of the car and Lauren slid into the front passenger seat. They were silent for the short journey, entertained by Lily's rendition of Twinkle Twinkle Little Star. When Kyra exited the car and trotted up her driveway, Lauren called after her, "Call me later. I mean it."

Chapter 8

Entering the house, adrenaline surged through Kyra's veins in anticipation of flight. She took the stairs two at a time and rapped on Liam's door. No reply. Good. She was definitely alone. Closing her bedroom door behind her, she quickly changed into jogging bottoms and a vest top – her slouchy clothes – and lay on her bed. Then, jumping up again, she picked up the wooden chair from in front of her desk and wedged it tightly under the door handle. For extra measure, she dragged her bedside table across the small room and pushed it up against the chair. That should do it.

Lying on her bed again, she stared up at the ceiling, and took deep breaths to calm herself after the burst of activity. When her heart returned to its normal pace, she closed her eyes and tried to focus on raising herself up off the bed.

Up, she willed herself silently. Go up.

Relaxing her body, she imagined the feeling of lifting up off the bed, floating up toward the ceiling. Nothing happened. Frustration rose inside her. What if she couldn't do it again? What if it wasn't real? What if she'd just imagined it, or if it had been nothing more than a daydream?

No, it was real. It was definitely real, she told herself firmly. She'd been wide awake when it happened. Her memory was crystal clear. She could do it again. She would do it again. She was sure of that now. She didn't know why she was so sure, but she knew it with as much certainty as she knew her own name.

Focus, she instructed herself. She tried a different tactic - tried to remember exactly what had happened the first time. Maybe she could recreate the experience, re-live it.

After dinner the previous day, Kyra had relaxed on her bed daydreaming about the upcoming under eighteen's night at the Beckridge Centre. She'd never been before and had never wanted to, seeing it as a place for the bitch brigade to hang out and show off. But Lauren's nagging had finally worked, and she had to admit she was actually starting to look forward to it. In her mind's eye she'd walked in to the hall looking and feeling amazing in the outfit Lauren had lent her (blue and purple checked shirt dress over purple leggings), with her hair and makeup newly styled. The music was loud, filling the hall, its beat filling her body, its rhythm coursing through her veins as if she was one with the music...

And that was it. That was when it had happened. She'd started buzzing all over, her arms first, then her legs and the rest of her body.

As she recalled the feeling, she realised it wasn't just a memory. It was happening again. There was that buzzing, filling her whole body, filling her head, filling her very core. She was light suddenly, as if made of cotton wool. All images of the Beckridge Centre dissolved completely from her mind and were replaced by white fuzz, like a snow storm.

She opened her eyes and could see the ceiling above her. She was slowly rising up toward it. Quelling the bubble of excitement that rose in her chest, she kept her mind blank, allowing no thoughts to form. When she was just inches below the ceiling she turned so she was upright and looked around the room. The forward planning this time had eliminated the element of surprise that had blinded her yesterday and she was determined to notice every little thing and to remain in control.

Her bedroom looked the same, yet different, like a special light was illuminating everything, a light with magical qualities. Her surroundings gleamed with spectacular clarity as if she was using a part of her eyes she'd never known existed. Colours seemed brighter yet more complex. Each hue appeared to be made of a million others. Objects looked solid yet seemed to be made of light itself. The air around her sparkled with miniscule globes of dancing light, twinkling like glitter. She spun in a slow circle, feeling an almost overwhelming sense of elation. She felt as if she shone like the air around her.

When she'd turned full circle she stopped. She was facing her bed, hovering in place like a humming bird. The sight in front of her probably should have been a shock, yet it wasn't. This was the part she'd not yet had a chance to tell Lauren. This was the part she knew would be pretty difficult to explain. Because Kyra was floating in the middle of her bedroom, but she was also looking at herself lying on the bed. She was in two places at once. The lying down Kyra appeared to be sleeping, but Kyra knew she wasn't asleep at all. She was just, well, kind of – vacant. Her eyes were closed, her chest rising and falling beneath the apple green vest top as she breathed.

She looked down at her second body now, the floating one, and lifted her hands in front of her face. Amazed, she realised she was semi transparent, kind of partly see-though. Like a ghost. Yet instinctively Kyra knew this didn't mean she was dead. She knew this not just because she'd done this yesterday. It was more than that, it was just a knowing. She didn't understand exactly what was happening but she felt safe.

Turning away from her resting body on the bed, she faced the window. The sky beckoned from beyond the pane of glass, its colour so intense it was mesmerising. She could see right into the blue, a kaleidescope of hues all moving together. She longed with every essence of her being to be amongst those colours, to move through them and feel the air whooshing past, but she was separated from the outdoors by a wall and her window wasn't open. Why hadn't she thought to open the window beforehand? She moved closer but was at a loss of what to do.

Nana Anna, please help me, she called silently.

Chapter 9

When Kyra was five, Nana Anna had told her she could always call on her for help. Nana Anna was dead at the time; it was the day of her funeral. Deemed too young to attend, Kyra had stayed home with Mrs. Dobbins from down the road. She'd just settled herself on the fluffy purple rug in the middle of her bedroom floor with a box of Lego, preparing to build a fairy castle, when something had caught her attention across the room. She'd looked up to see Nana Anna sitting on the edge of her bed, smiling down at her.

Kyra had yelped and squeezed her eyes closed.

"Are you really there?" she'd whispered, not daring to look.

"Yes, I'm really here, Pudding," Nana Anna had replied, her voice soft and warm like Kyra's favourite blanket. Kyra had peeked with one eye and had seen that her Nana was indeed still there.

"Oh," she'd squeaked. "Hi." She'd opened the other eye tentatively.

"Hello, Kitten." Nana Anna's lips hadn't moved when she had spoken. The words had just appeared in Kyra's head like magic.

"Are you still dead?" Kyra had asked, thoroughly confused.

"Nobody really dies, my Sweet Princess. We just move on to a place where we don't need our bodies anymore."

Kyra remembered the black cat purring contentedly on Nana Anna's lap. She'd recognised him immediately. It was Sooty, her

Nana's cherished pet who'd been squished by a lorry just before Nana Anna got ill. She had been delighted to see him in one piece again and reunited with his beloved owner.

"But you do have a body. I can see it," she'd stated.

When she'd studied Nana Anna more closely, however, she'd noticed her body was different; kind of light, almost see-through. That wasn't the only difference. The last few times Kyra had seen her grandmother alive, in that stinky nursing home, she'd looked like a deflated balloon, more shrunken and curled up every time they'd visited. But when she'd appeared to five year old Kyra, she'd looked just like the big cuddly Nana Anna that Kyra remembered from before, in her cheerful flowery purple dress instead of sad white hospital robes, with her hair all big and curly instead of a few wisps clinging to a flaky scalp.

"You're right, Darling. I do have a body, but it's not the same as yours. This is just so you can see me...so I can talk to you. You see, I'm here to help you."

Kyra had been confused, and distracted by the drifts of old music she could hear behind her Nana's voice, and a man singing.

"What do you mean, help me? What do I need help with?" she'd asked, shifting onto her knees to relieve her numb bum.

"You don't need help with anything right now, Sugar Plum. But you must always remember that you're special, and you're here for a very special reason. You don't need to think about that right now. I just wanted you to know that I'm still here with you. I will always be just a thought away."

Chapter 10

Kyra felt her grandmother's presence in the room before she saw her. Today she barely noticed the twangy Elvis Presley music that always accompanied her Nana's arrival as she turned to see her smiling Nana in her usual spot on the edge of the bed.

"I did it!" Kyra exclaimed, somehow aware that Nana Anna had been waiting patiently for this day for years.

"You did, sweetheart. Yes you did," her Nana smiled knowingly. By now Kyra was used to holding their conversations silently, in the mind. She'd long since stopped speaking her side of the exchange out loud. It caused strange reactions when people happened to be within earshot, as she'd discovered in some very embarrassing past incidents.

Kyra felt closer than ever to Nana Anna now. Connected. It was a wonderful feeling.

"So this is what it's like for you? I always wondered," She laughed.

"Well yes, Pumpkin, this is what it's like sometimes, when I'm here in your world. And isn't it beautiful? Now imagine this but a million times more stunning – that's what it's like in some worlds I've visited."

It was rare for Nana Anna to divulge information about what she did or where she went when she wasn't with Kyra, and Kyra loved hearing these occasional little snippets.

Wow, just how many worlds are there out there? she wondered.

"More than you could ever imagine," Nana Ana replied with a laugh. "But you have a lot more to do in this one before you experience any others!"

"I know," Kyra said, although she didn't really, and wanted to ask Nana Anna to explain. But first she needed to clarify exactly what was happening to be sure she understood.

"So I'm guessing that this is my spirit body, right? Like, I've left the vehicle for a while to have a little wander around?" she asked, using the car analogy her Nana had used all those years ago.

"Kind of, my Princess. You've just discovered that it's also possible to travel in this world without using your physical body. Now you're travelling in your light body," she explained.

"This is so cool! Ok, so how do I get outside? I mean, I can't open the window or the door."

"No you can't. You're right, because they're solid and you're light. You're not physical any more, but all these objects you see around you are. You're still in the same space as they are. But you don't experience them as physical objects like you do when you're in your physical body. If you tried to move them you would feel them, but your hand would simply move right through them."

Kyra wasn't at all sure she understood, but she would take the word of the expert. She let her Nana continue without interrupting. "For that same reason you could just move right through the window if you wanted, or the wall. But you don't need to do that."

"I don't?" Kyra asked, moving closer to the wall. She wasn't really listening now. She was trying to get her head round what she'd just heard – she could walk through walls? This she had to try! She reached out a tentative hand and felt it touch the wall, felt the smooth coolness of the cream paint. But her hand didn't stop there. It kept going right on through. She felt the plaster and then the roughness of the brick against her fingers. She kept on pushing her hand through until she felt just air on her fingertips and the warmth of the sinking sun.

"Oh, My Giddy Aunt!" she exclaimed. This was awesome. Her

arm was literally going through the wall. She pushed forward until her elbow disappeared. Taking another step closer, she leaned forward with her head and felt the tip of her nose touch the paint and then the plaster beyond. The rest of her face followed and she could clearly see every fibre of the materials that made up the wall. She kept on pushing forward until her face was in the open air – the outside world right there before her in all its glory.

Quickly pulling herself back inside she spun to face Nana Anna who was still sitting on the bed stroking Sooty, watching Kyra with amusement.

"This is incredible. I can like – go through anything? That's fantastic!" The possibilities were only just beginning to dawn on Kyra. "But wait a minute. You said I don't need to do that. What did you mean?" she asked.

"Honey Bunch, things work differently when you're in your light body. Everything is faster than on the physical level. Everything is just a thought away."

Kyra didn't get it.

"What do you mean?"

"Just what I said – everything is just a thought away. You want to go somewhere, just think of it. Think of going there. Intend to go there. And you will."

Kyra was dubious, but she was willing to give it a go.

Okay, where to go? Suddenly her mind was blank.

"How about your school?" Nana Anna suggested. And an image of the sprawling red brick building presented itself in Kyra's head.

Well, it'll do for a test, she thought. Ok, I intend to go there. I want to go to school. She repeated it over and over like a mantra and visualised the large black iron gates.

Suddenly she was rushing through a tunnel of colour and swirling noise and then there she was – swooping through the iron gates of the school – exactly as she'd imagined. This just couldn't get any better, Kyra thought, as she zoomed around the playground, flying up high until she was nearly touching the clouds, and then diving down low, the warm air rushing past.

She soared over the school field, building up speed like she'd been unable to do in the confines of her room. Circling the perimeter of the field, she glided low enough to feel the leaves of the trees brushing against her hands. Going faster still she swept over the patchwork fields that lay beyond the school. She was one with the wind and the hazy afternoon light. She was living her dream.

As she returned toward the school, a group of kids in football gear caught her attention in the car park down below. Floating slowly closer, she was nervous, but pretty sure they wouldn't be able to see her. Moving right up in front of them, she flew in a circle around the group that she now recognised as the "cool" gang of the year sevens. Not one of them so much as batted an eyelid.

She was invisible! This was just unbelievable – she could go where she wanted and nobody could see her. She could fly through walls, through doors, through windows. The possibilities were endless. Looking at the boys in front of her, she considered flying through one of them to see what it was like, wondering if she would see their internal organs, their blood, their cells, wondering if they would notice. But no, that was just way too weird. She shivered with disgust at the thought.

Looking toward the school she decided to go through the wall of the building instead. She could fly right into the staff room and nobody would know. She could hear what the teachers really talk about after the students went home! She chose the wall near the office entrance which would bring her out right next to the staff room. Turning to the right she approached the wall slowly, cautiously, still slightly apprehensive about just zooming full speed through the solid brick, just in case.

She was about to float through the wall when a movement to her left caught her eye. A figure was walking toward her, a beautiful girl moving with all the grace of a swan, gliding along the path. Her skin was a deep brown, her black hair swinging around her head in tiny plaits. Kyra watched, transfixed, and it was only as the girl moved closer to her that Kyra noticed she was semi-transparent, just like Nana Anna. Just like her too. And then she realised the girl

45

wasn't walking at all. She was hovering at least a foot above the ground. Kyra froze, uncomprehending.

As the girl's head turned, her gaze fixed on Kyra. She looked right into Kyra's eyes. She smiled. She can see me, Kyra realised. Panic burst inside her, overwhelming her. I have to get out of here. I have to go. Now. The scene in front of her faded, the school, the girl. A rush of coloured lights embraced her, wrapping her in a whirlpool. Then everything was still. Everything was white.

She opened her eyes, and saw her ceiling above her – right up where it was supposed to be. She was back in her physical body, back on her bed. She wiggled her toes, then her fingers. They felt heavy. She felt heavy. Sitting up, she looked around and realised everything looked dull and plain in comparison to how things appeared when she was in her light body. Everything felt slow and dense, like being underwater. Nana Anna was still right there on the end of the bed.

"There was a girl at school, Nana Anna. And she saw me. I think she was a ghost. I mean a spirit, like you." The words tumbled out in a rush as Kyra pulled herself upright.

"Sweetheart, she was human, alive, just like you," Nana Anna replied calmly. And then she responded to Kyra's questioning look. "I saw her, Munchkin. I was there too. I went with you."

Kyra was surprised by this. She hadn't noticed her Nana's presence. But right now she was more concerned about the girl at the school.

"What do you mean she was human? I don't understand. How did she see me?"

"You know, Kyra, this will come as a surprise to you, but what you can do - flying as you call it - there are others who can do it too. And now and again you're bound to come across each other. When you're flying you're on the same energy level, so you're visible to each other."

Kyra struggled to take this in. There were people flying around all over the place? She supposed it was quite egotistical to assume she was the only person who could do it. Kyra thought about the girl's expression, her little smile, the kindness in her eyes. She didn't look surprised or freaked out. She looked like she'd definitely been doing it a while.

"But why? Why can we do this?"

"Now that's the right question, my dear. Unfortunately it's also the question I can't give you an answer to. You're going to have to figure that one out for yourself. But remember, everything has a reason, even if it's not immediately obvious."

Kyra was calming down now and realised she had no cause to be worried or upset. She was just sorry she'd cut short her flying experience so suddenly. Oh well, she knew now that she could do it whenever she wanted. Within the last half hour she'd entered a magical new world and gained the kind of freedom most fourteen-year-olds could only dream of. She smiled, engulfed in the tingling memories of her experience, the glow of magic still clinging to her.

"So, my darling, how does it feel to fly?" Nana Anna asked.

"There are no words Nana Anna – there are simply no words to describe it."

Kyra was so caught up in the magnificent memory of her flying experience that she barely noticed her Nana fading and blowing her a kiss, before disappearing into thin air.

A knock at her bedroom door brought her back into the real world with a jolt.

Chapter 11

The dread that clung to the Visitor when he returned to his body was as unpleasant as the film of sweat that coated his skin. The first visit to a future event was always the hardest one, the most frustrating. He couldn't get close enough to see anything of importance. The visuals were vague and out of focus, the colours were dim, muddy. There were people but no faces, voices but no words. It was like he'd been taken to a time that hadn't properly formed yet. This visit had been no different, so unspecific it was virtually useless. It had told him nothing.

Grasping desperately to every small detail, he retrieved the notebook and pen he kept with him at all times and started scribbling what he could remember. Experience had taught him that even the most seemingly inconsequential detail could be of utmost importance further down the line.

Outside, dark. Rain, rumbling sound: thunder? At least two people maybe more. Sadness. Danger. Death.

Yes, sadness was the emotion of this visit. There was always an emotion and it was rarely a positive one, grief, despair, panic, fear, and other varying degrees of the same theme. The sadness that had returned with him from this visit weighed down his heart like an anchor and it would remain there until the situation came to a conclusion. But it wasn't the sadness that had caused his dread.

It was the danger, and the responsibility to divert it that had just landed on his shoulders. Yet there was nothing he could do but wait for his next visit.

Death was coming, and it was his job to intervene.

Chapter 12

"I'll be there in a minute," Kyra called, glancing at the clock on her wall, shocked to see that it was nearly five already. She hadn't got anything ready for supper yet. Standing up in a hurry, she remembered the furniture she'd shoved in front of the door and quickly dragged the bedside table back into place, making quite a racket in the process.

"Kyra, what on Earth are you doing in there?" Liam asked and pushed open the door, sending the wooden chair she'd wedged there tumbling. Kyra quickly assumed an innocent hand on hip position.

"Oh, nothing. I was just trying out a different furniture arrangement. And anyway, since when are you allowed to come barging in here without permission?" Her face burned as it always did when she told a fib. She was the world's worst liar. She crossed her arms across her chest and scowled, slipping quickly into attack mode to divert attention from her own activities.

"I didn't exactly barge in. I just opened the door. Well I can see you're in a great mood," he said sarcastically, sweeping his long mop of brown hair out of his eyes as he talked. "I just wondered where you were. You're usually downstairs, that's all." He held his hands up as if in surrender.

"You mean you wondered why there's no dinner cooking? Well I'm not the paid help, you know. Whatever happened to our household agreement to take it in turns to cook? So far it seems to be my turn every day! What have you been up to today anyway? Got a job yet?" She stared defiantly at her brother who was slouching casually against her doorframe, his tall body clad in black skinny jeans and a black waistcoat.

"I told you, sis, I'm working on something important," he replied. "You could say I'm doing a community service." He gave her one of his weird smiles and turned and sauntered toward the stairs.

Kyra didn't bother trying to work out what he was going on about; he seemed to get odder every day. Sometimes she wondered if he acted that way just to wind her up. Or maybe he was taking drugs. She shook her head, not wanting to entertain that possibility.

"Oh, and by the way, I already put dinner on to cook. Pasta tuna bake. It's in the oven," Liam called as he descended the stairs.

Wow, if he is on something, I hope he keeps taking it, Kyra thought.

Chapter 13

Entering the kitchen through the back door, the first thing Noah noticed was the lingering aroma of the spaghetti bolognaise they'd enjoyed for dinner. The second thing he noticed was the note on the counter.

Leftovers in fridge. Thought you might be hungry after all that hard work. Movie and popcorn tomorrow? Love Mum x

He smiled to himself. Saturday night was movie night for the Pinkertons, and the only night his mum flatly refused to work. When he was little they'd snuggle up on the sofa, cocooned together in her huge duvet which smelt of flowers and sunshine, gorging themselves on popcorn and milkshakes. Sometimes he'd glance over and catch her watching him, instead of the film. Her smile would make him glow. These days Noah knew movie night was more for his mum's benefit than his, and he only wished her big puffy duvet still had the power to wrap him in a world of security and snugness.

Glancing at the clock he realised he must have only just missed her. When he'd nipped next door to update some scripts for Monkey Cove, he'd only planned to be an hour; but time had somehow run away from him. He hated coming home to an empty house, and the first thing he did, as always, was to make sure all the doors were locked and the curtains closed, despite the fact it was still light outside.

He retrieved the bowl of leftover spag-bol from the fridge and set it in the microwave to reheat. The sudden noise sounded ridiculously loud in the silence of the house, causing his nerves to jangle. Berating himself, he pulled open the microwave door and decided to eat it cold.

As he sat down in the lounge to eat, remote control in hand, the phone rang. The shrill sound made him jump and he looked toward the phone as if it were an enemy, self aware, out to get him, and then turned away again and upped the volume on the television. He stared at a gardening program without really seeing it. The bowl of food on his lap remained untouched.

The phone rang again when he was binning the food, telling himself he wasn't as hungry as he'd thought. It rang a third time when he was washing up, and a fourth time when he was brushing his teeth. Lying in bed watching The Apprentice, he told himself for the gazillionth time he would get through this. It would end one day, he just had to stay strong and not let Marco win. Then he told himself he was letting Marco win by even giving him brain space and vowed to stop thinking about him. Just a few minutes later he realised he had no idea what tonight's task was on The Apprentice, but he knew it had been exactly ten minutes since the phone last rang. He sighed.

He wondered if it was possible for a person to be driven insane by this kind of harassment. It certainly felt possible. He wondered again if he was wrong by taking no action against Marco. But what could he do? Even if he didn't go to his mum and chose to talk to someone else instead – the police, his teacher, whomever – ultimately it would get back to his mum. It had to. He was a minor and she was in charge of him, and he just couldn't put her through that. He owed her too much.

She'd been eight months pregnant when his father had died in a car accident at just twenty-three years old. He'd been rushing to the hospital where his wife had been admitted with labour pains. Ironically just as she was being sent back home with a diagnosis of false labour, he was being rushed into the same hospital in an ambulance, already dead. Everything they'd built together, their hopes and dreams of a family, a future, wiped out in an instant. She'd talked about him constantly over the years, sharing stories and laughing at memories as if they'd happened just last week instead of years ago.

Noah had lapped the stories up with an unquenchable thirst and she'd painted the tales over and over adding more details each time, more clarity, to the point that now the memories felt like his own.

Twelve minutes now since the phone last rang and he allowed himself to drift into a daydream about his father, to wonder how different things would be if he was here. His dad, the fireman, the hero of his childhood fantasies. Would he have sorted Marco DiCarmello out? Would Noah's mum live instead of just surviving, just getting by for Noah's sake, as she had been doing since the day her husband was ripped from her life? He remembered asking her once how she'd coped with the sadness of losing someone she loved so much, and she'd told him it was the feeling of somebody she loved just as much moving and kicking inside her that had pulled her through. She always kept her tone light, but he could read between the lines. He could see in her eyes that without a baby to look after she would have drowned in her own grief.

Fourteen minutes had passed now since the phone rang and Noah had given up pretending not to count. He was scared. For some reason the phone not ringing was even worse than it ringing. Impulsively grabbing the handset, he dialled 1471 to see what number had called him. The scientist in him knew that he could eliminate fear altogether if it was an innocent wrong number, or even somebody he knew calling and then getting distracted, hanging up before he answered.

But no, it was number withheld. It was bound to be Marco and his fears were definitely founded. He pressed the disconnect button, but before he could put the handset back the deafening ring cried out in his hand. Startled, he screamed and threw the phone as if it had bitten him.

Curling into the corner of the wall, he hugged his knees to his chest, shaking all over, not taking his eyes from the phone. Then resolve surged within him almost as quickly as the fear that had attacked him; and without even knowing he was going to do it, he felt himself jump to his feet and grab the handset, as if he were a puppet, controlled by an unknown master.

"Hello?" he shouted into the phone, surprising himself with the strength in his voice. "Hello?" Still no response. "Look, I know who this is and if you think I'm scared..."

But he didn't get to finish the sentence. A soft click told him the caller had hung up.

Returning to his bed he pulled the covers up around him and turned up the volume on the T.V. in an attempt to drown out the dread that filled him. The walls of the room seemed to be creeping closer, closing in on him until he felt he wanted to scream, his heart racing, panic rising. The noise was doing nothing to help, only making him even jumpier. So he turned the T.V. off, but not the light – the light always stayed on at night time. He welcomed the calmness of the silence as he curled himself into a ball under the covers, begging sleep to come quickly. Concentrating on the familiar sounds of the old house settling, he labelled each one, reassuring himself they were all noises that belonged – nothing that would indicate an intruder.

Soon enough the safety of sleep wrapped its gentle blanket around him, but not for long. A new sound, unidentifiable, intruded the depths of slumber. A tapping, erratic but repetitive, tugged him further and further from sleep until he was fully awake and so full of fear he wanted to cry. Sitting upright he realised the noise was coming from his window – every tap like a gunshot. Lying back down he pulled the covers up around his chin and stared intently at the ceiling, numbing himself against the thoughts and possibilities that were trying to claim his mind.

It went on for about five minutes. Five long minutes. And then it suddenly stopped just like that. The silence didn't make him feel any better. His thoughts were suddenly filled with possible horrific scenarios, his body stiff with terror. He didn't dare move an inch, couldn't even begin to think about the possibility of sleeping again.

There was a sudden thump on the wooden front door, so loud it sounded as if a rhino was trying to break in. He would have screamed if his fear had allowed him. Panic returned and Noah was torn between calling the police and climbing into his wardrobe, although he resolved to do neither. He wouldn't bring this pain to his mother and he wouldn't be a coward either. Sitting up in bed he stared at his bedroom door and waited, although he didn't know what he was waiting for.

But that was it. One solitary thump. Noah stayed in that position for a long time until exhausted sleep eventually claimed him.

Chapter 14

"I want to do it."

It was far from the response Kyra had expected. She could tell Lauren was serious from the earnest look in her huge blue eyes.

"What? No questions? I tell you I came out of my body, walked through walls, and flew to school and back, and you have nothing to say except that you want to do it?"

It was Friday morning and the girls had met even earlier than the previous day and walked a completely different route to school. It added about twenty minutes to their journey but it was worth it. Kyra had reached the end of the story without being forced to leave it on a cliff-hanger this time. She'd dashed through the tale with such speed that the words were almost tripping over each other. Lauren had listened intently, open mouthed, until the final full stop.

"It sounds so awesome. I really want to do it. You can teach me." Lauren looked at Kyra pleadingly.

"Well, I don't know. I mean, I don't think it's something anyone can just do. I think it's kind of something you're born with, like being able to draw really well or something."

"But Nana Anna said it was just a case of leaving the physical body and travelling in the light body, right?" Lauren made it sound so simple. "And we all have these light bodies right? I mean, not just a select few people? And she did say that there are other people out there doing it, like the girl you saw." Lauren put a forward a strong argument, and Kyra could imagine her following her mother's footsteps into a career in law instead of the acting profession she dreamed of.

"I guess. I mean, yeah, we do," Kyra stuttered. She could see where Lauren was coming from, and where she was going.

"So I could learn to do it – if you tell me exactly how you did it, and if I practise enough? I mean, like you said, not everybody is born being able to draw really well – but surely anybody can if they practise hard enough?"

"Well, I suppose. I don't see why it wouldn't be possible."

"Oh my God, Kyra, just imagine the adventures we could have together. Just think what we could do. We could spy on people from school, we could visit each other in the middle of the night without anyone knowing we'd even left our houses – we could do anything."

Kyra was smiling too now. Lauren's enthusiasm was so infectious, and she had to admit it did sound like fun. Although she still wasn't convinced she'd be able to teach Lauren how to do it, surely it couldn't hurt to try?

"All right Lauren. Let's do it. I'll do it," she nodded resolutely.

"Oh my God! Yay!" Lauren screamed and hugged Kyra, jumping up and down at the same time until both of them were giggling. "You are the best friend ever!"

"When? When shall we do it?" Lauren asked when their moment of craziness had finally subsided. "Please say tonight, please, please, please," she begged comically.

"Well it is Friday...how do you fancy sleeping over tonight?"

"I love you, Miss Sutton! You're seriously the best!" Lauren cried. She'd already pulled out her mobile and started tapping a text message, asking her mum for permission, her thumbs moving fluently across the keys.

The day was as fine as the previous one, full of promise for a magnificent summer, and they enjoyed strolling along in silence, lost in their own daydreams of flying adventures, until Lauren's message tone pulled them back down to Earth. Looking down at the display she gave a whoop of delight.

"We're on! Mum says it's ok. This is gonna be so cool. Ok, so after school we'll head to my house so I can grab some stuff. Then back to yours and the fun begins!" She was doing that little hopping on the spot thing she always did.

"Sounds like a plan," Kyra agreed as they set off once more, speeding up their pace, eager now to get through the day.

After a few moments of walking in silence, Lauren turned to her friend. "Did it freak you out? When you saw the girl, I mean. Did she definitely see you? It's so weird to think there are people out there just flying around and we can't see them! And who do you think she was? I mean, what was she doing at the school?" As usual she fired off a whole string of questions without waiting for any answers.

"I have no idea why she was at the school. There's a netball game coming up against Farring High isn't there? I bet she's on their team, coming to check out the competition." Kyra smiled, thinking of all the mischief she could now get up to herself. "She definitely saw me though, and it did freak me out at first, yeah, totally. I mean it's weird. But I'll probably never see the girl again in my life." Kyra kicked a stone as she walked, unconcerned.

Chapter 15

Just ten minutes later Kyra discovered exactly how wrong she could be.

"I'd like to introduce you to your new classmates, Ray and Crystal Hudson, who've moved here all the way from Indiana in the United States of America," Mrs Saunders announced grandly during class registration.

Kyra turned her head along with the rest of the class to see the new students who were loitering in the doorway. She found herself staring into a very familiar face smiling brightly next to a boy who could only be her brother. Spinning hastily back to face the front, Kyra sunk low in her chair and stared down at her desk, hiding behind her hair.

Oh God, what do I do? Will she recognise me? What if she blabs in front of the class? Everyone will know what a freak I am! The questions were vying for attention in her mind and she didn't know what else to do but hide. She was panicked at the thought of coming face to face with this person who knew what she could do. A murmur rose in the room as people gawped at the new students as if they were some kind of freak show.

"Oh cool. Twins!" Lauren whispered loudly. "Oh Lordy, Kyra check him out. Now that's what I call hot!" She turned back toward Kyra, and immediately noticed the change in her friend's demeanour.

"Hey, what's up?"

"Nothing, I'll tell you later," Kyra whispered back. She saw movement from the corner of her eye as the twins made their way toward an empty desk near the front of the classroom.

Slouching down even further, she pretended to study her nails. Damn, what am I going to do if she sees me? she asked herself again, although she knew it was more a case of when, rather than if. She wouldn't be able to hide forever. And that's some big-ass coincidence anyway, she thought, confused. Someone who can fly turning up in my class the same week I discover I can.

Lauren gasped, suddenly making the connection. "Oh geez, it's her isn't it?" she whispered.

Kyra nodded solemnly.

She very nearly made it all the way to the end of the school day without coming face to face with Crystal. But not quite. It was the last period of the day, French class. The tables in the classroom were arranged in a U shape around the room. Lauren was sitting to her left, but as the classroom filled up, the seat to her right remained empty. She was mentally willing someone to sit there. Anyone. Anyone other than Crystal, that is.

She almost didn't dare look when she felt a presence at her side and heard the sound of the plastic orange chair scraping across the floor like nails across a blackboard.

"Hi there. I hope it's okay for me to sit here?" Crystal asked, her voice soft and mellow.

Kyra reluctantly turned toward her and smiled, bracing herself for the gasp of recognition.

"Of course, it's fine," she mumbled, fiddling nervously with her pen as she lifted her eyes to her new classmate, resigned to the unavoidable encounter. She might as well get it over and done with. Part of her had even started to wonder throughout the day if they could become friends, share their experiences.

Crystal beamed a radiant smile. "I'm Crystal, nice to meet you," she said formally and held out her hand to shake. There was no recognition in the girl's striking face whatsoever.

"I'm Kyra, nice to meet you too." They shook hands, Kyra feeling a little silly, extremely confused and, she reluctantly admitted to herself, slightly disappointed.

"Hi, I'm Lauren," Lauren offered, leaning back on her chair and extending her own hand behind Kyra's back. Kyra noticed her friend scanning the class furtively, no doubt seeking the other twin, who was nowhere to be seen.

"Well hi, Lauren. You have such beautiful hair," Crystal gushed, her American accent instantly making her seem older and more sophisticated than any of the other girls in their class.

"Oh gee, thanks," Lauren gushed, thrilled with the compliment, although still disappointed about the absence of Crystal's brother.

Further conversation was impeded by the arrival of Mr. Dupére. Kyra couldn't relax; she didn't understand what was going on. Was Crystal just pretending not to recognise her? Maybe it wasn't her? she wondered. Or maybe she can fly like me but didn't actually see me? The questions were endless and remained unanswered.

She started doodling in her notebook, avoiding eye contact with the French teacher in the hopes that she wouldn't be picked on to demonstrate her ability to order a three course meal in Paris. The only thing she hated more than speaking in front of a large group of people was speaking in French in front of a large group of people. Then she had not only her blushing and shaky voice to contend with, but also her inability to sound even remotely continental.

Crystal, in contrast, spoke with an almost perfect French accent, as they discovered when she was called upon to introduce herself en Francais. It didn't surprise Kyra – it seemed to fit with the elegance that polished Crystal's every word and movement.

"My grandparents spoke French. They were Creole, from Louisiana originally," she revealed by way of explanation. "They moved north when they were young but insisted their children and grandchildren would all continue speaking the language. We've spoken it in my house for as long as I can remember."

Crystal was the most interesting thing to have happened at school for a long time and the class seemed to hang on her every word, intrigued by a student who seemed to actually flaunt her intelligence with pride, yet could by no means be classed as either smug or a geek. She was an entirely new breed, the likes of which Cranley High had never seen. Mr. Dupére could barely conceal his delight and gave Crystal the somewhat dubious honour of being called upon to demonstrate the correct pronunciation of every single phrase they learned for the rest of the afternoon. Crystal seemed only too happy to comply, and somehow managed to still seem cool. The girl was an anomaly.

Kyra's concerns about the flying incident with Crystal gradually dimmed, and she allowed herself to relax a little and enjoy the anticipation of the evening ahead. Sleepovers were always fun, full of the latest DVDs, the latest gossip, and plenty of junk food; but tonight would have the added ingredient of flying. She wondered if Lauren really could learn to fly. That would be incredible. She visualised them soaring together over the rooftops toward the beach, across the English Channel, and into the glittering twilight until there was only endless water as far as the eye could see. She could smell the sea salt in the ocean breeze and feel the cool spray from the crashing waves as they dived down low, teasing the sea gulls.

The bell to signal end of class and the ensuing orchestra of chairs scraping loudly across the floor tugged her rudely out of her daydream. She stood and began gathering her things. Looking down she noticed her notebook was covered in sketches of birds and wings and an elaborate pattern of swirls. Quickly tearing off the sheet, she balled it up in her fist and shoved it deep inside her bag.

"So, we'll see you around, Crystal," Lauren said as they made for the door, and Crystal gave them a little wave.

"Hold up a minute Kyra, if you don't mind," Mr. Dupére called, as Kyra rolled her eyes in Lauren's direction before turning to face the teacher.

"Fancy a takeaway tomorrow? Chinese, Indian?" He smiled brightly, completely oblivious to the sniggers coming from the stragglers still leaving the classroom. Kyra felt her face burn with embarrassment. No, she wasn't being hit on by the youngest and best looking teacher in the school. He was in fact her soon-to-be stepfather, the boy toy her mother had run off with after taking an evening French course he'd taught, to "experience more culture." Well, she'd certainly experienced more something. For the last year she'd been playing house with Kyra's French teacher as if they were young sweethearts, when in reality she was fifteen years his senior and he was only eleven years older than Kyra herself.

It was humiliating, but Kyra's sulking campaign which had lasted for months had resulted in nothing more than her own growing frustration and had seemed to have no effect on their relationship whatsoever. Eventually Kyra's father had asked her to give her mum a break, to let her be happy. At first Kyra had been livid. She'd actually been trying to stick up for her dad and that was the thanks she got? But after talking it over with first Lauren and then Noah, she'd come to understand that maybe her father had actually been relieved when his wife had left him. After all, even Kyra could see how high maintenance her mother was. And now he could sit at his computer for as many hours as he wanted without cutting remarks or loaded sighs. He could have his hair cut, or not, as he pleased; and he didn't have to attend "drinks" or "dinners" with plastic people he couldn't stand.

So on balance, Kyra had concluded that if her dad was happy and if her mum was happy, then she might as well try to be happy too. For the last few weeks she'd taken to spending every other Saturday night with her mother and Dupére at the flat they shared in town, and even helping them with their wedding plans. She had to admit, being nice to them was much easier than being miserable all the time, and it was kind of fun to have two homes. However, Mr. Dupére (or Piérre as he insisted she call him outside of school), who'd been determined to turn them into one big happy family from the beginning, was over-the-top thrilled by her change of heart, and had started being so ridiculously nice it was almost creepy. What a complete try-hard!

"Yeah, takeaway's cool, whatever," she muttered and sped out the door before he could respond, Lauren nearly collapsing with silent giggles as they rushed through the corridor.

Chapter 16

His shoulder hurt and his white school shirt was ruined by streaks of grass and mud, not to mention drops of blood from the scratch on his cheek. However, none of these minor annoyances came even close to what he would have suffered if he hadn't dived into the bushes when he'd seen Marco up ahead.

Eventually Noah emerged from his leafy hideout, but only when he was absolutely certain Marco and his crew were long gone. The rest of his journey home was an exercise in caution. Like something out of a spy film, he scurried rather than walked, checking carefully around every corner and glancing over his shoulder constantly. The whole time the same thought was screaming for his attention, the same thought that had been gaining volume over the past days, maybe even weeks: This has to stop.

As he reached Saffron Road he stopped on the corner, hiding behind the post box. Peering down the road he scanned every front garden to make sure there was nobody lying in wait for him. Nothing. But still he stiffened with fear as he approached his house, glancing nervously into the branches of the conifers that lined the short pathway, and pushing away the unwelcome vision that flashed into his mind...Marco sitting in wait in his lounge, grinning....*NO, stop it!*

Forcing himself to focus, he fumbled in the front pocket of his school bag for his key. And if Marco is sitting in the lounge waiting for him, where is his mum who should be there preparing dinner? *NO, STOP IT!* He wouldn't allow himself to sink further into this spiral of terror.

This was completely out of control now. His mind had taken a playground bully and made him into an unstoppable monster. Even though the rational part of his brain knew this, the fear seemed to be in complete control of him anyway. He wondered if he was going mad. Finally managing to get the key into the lock with shaking hands, he pushed the door open and shouted, "Hi Mum, I'm home." Swinging the door closed behind him, he only realised he was holding his breath when his mum's reply sailed down the hallway.

"Hi, darling."

With a sigh he ran up the stairs and changed into jeans and a T-shirt in record time, stuffing his soiled shirt into his school bag to deal with later. Inspecting the scratch on his cheek in the bathroom mirror, he was relieved to see it was only minor. And after wiping away the dried blood, it was barely visible and could be easily explained away.

Back downstairs, he wandered into the kitchen where his mum was chopping onions.

"How was your day?" she asked over her shoulder as he entered.

The room was bright and cheerful. Everything was normal. Everything was fine. Everything was in stark contrast to how it would be in just a few hours when she left for work.

"Yeah, not bad," he lied.

"Oh good," she answered distractedly. "Listen, I'm sorry, Noah, but I have to go in early today. Susie called in sick and I said I'd cover from five. You just need to let this simmer for about half an hour and cook yourself some rice. You know how to do that, right?"

"Yes, mum. I'm not a baby. I'll be fine," he answered, trying not to let the dread that hit him in the pit of his stomach show in his face.

One thing was for sure, he couldn't face another night here alone. He made a decision right there and then that he would leave the house when his mum did. He'd been planning to go next door and work on Monkey Cove later anyway. So he'd just go a little earlier than planned. And if he happened to fall asleep on the sofa and end up spending the night, well, he was pretty sure nobody would mind.

"You're a good boy," she said as she washed her hands and then she turned toward him as she dried them on a tea-towel. "Oh, Noah, what happened to your cheek?" she asked, rushing over to examine the scratch.

"Just an accident in P.E. It's nothing," he said, hating himself for all lies he seemed to be telling her these days.

Chapter 17

"It's not working. I can't do it!" Lauren moaned.

Kyra opened her eyes and looked up to where Lauren was lying on her bed, flat on her back with her eyes scrunched closed. "It's not going to work as long as you keep talking. You have to be completely relaxed and focussed," she said again.

"But I've been trying to be relaxed and focussed for nearly an hour now. It's not working," Lauren wailed and stomped her feet against the mattress in frustration.

"Come on, one more try," Kyra instructed. "Now take a deep breath, and think of your favourite dance song. Not the words, just the beat. Feel the rhythm. Let it fill up your body, and just lie like that for a while." As she spoke, Kyra followed her own guidance, lying on her back and relaxing, although she found it easy to spontaneously fly now and didn't actually need to try.

"Now imagine your body is the music. Imagine you feel light, and tingly. And then just lift up." Kyra rose up out of her own body and spun around eagerly to face her friend, hopeful that it might have worked this time. But no, she couldn't see Lauren's light body, only her physical one lying on the bed. And her physical face, which was scrunched so tightly in concentration she looked like she might burst a blood vessel. Kyra laughed silently at the sight, wondering what else she could try, when she suddenly sensed a presence.

It felt like when Nana Anna appeared, but different, more intense.

Spinning to face the window, she could see him there, right there outside looking in, and she was mesmerised. The boy before her was obviously flying too, his light body partially transparent, as was hers; but there was something about him, something different. He was radiant; his olive skin emitting a golden light. His hair, too, shimmered and even his blue eyes, piercing right through her, appeared to exude pure gold light, the exact same hue as the wheat of her dreams. But it was more than just the perfection of his appearance that kept her transfixed. She simply couldn't tear her eyes away from his because she knew him. That made no sense, even to her, but she was drawn to him so strongly that when he faded and disappeared, she felt an immediate sense of loss, of mourning. It was only then she registered Lauren's voice and the fact that her friend was shaking her shoulder vigorously.

"Ky...Ky, come on, get up. What's wrong with you?" Lauren asked, concern etched in her face. Kyra slipped back into her body and sat up, making Lauren jump. "Holy Mother of...you scared the life out of me then!"

"I'm sorry. I was just...just trying to think of another way to do this," Kyra improvised.

"And did you come up with anything?" Lauren looked hopeful.

"Yes, I decided you're right. We need a break," Kyra said, her mind elsewhere. She'd decided not to mention the boy to Lauren. There were just too many questions. Who was he? What was he doing here? And why hadn't she been scared? A strange boy looking in her bedroom window should have terrified her, but it didn't. Instead she found herself stealing sideways glances at the spot where he'd been, hoping he'd return.

"But I don't want to stop," Lauren said, alarmed, and sat on the bed.

"A minute ago you were complaining about how long we've been doing this and now you shout at me when I suggest a break – what do you want?" Kyra asked, exasperated.

"I just want to be able to do it. I really thought it would just happen, I thought it was like meant to be. I just want to make it work," Lauren pouted, and Kyra felt like a bitch for being snappy.

"Lauren, it will work, ok? We will keep going until we make it work," she insisted with a lot more conviction than she felt.

"Honest?" Lauren looked hopeful.

"Honest. We're just trying too hard. We need a short break to calm ourselves." And to work out some different tactics, she added silently. Clearly nothing she'd tried so far had worked.

"I agree," Lauren grinned, going from sulky to cheerful in about 0.2 seconds. "Refreshments. That's what we need. Very sugary refreshments. Oooh, do you have choccy biccies? And orange juice? I think that will definitely help!" She was on her feet already, pulling Kyra up from the floor.

"Yes to both. Although I see absolutely no scientific reason why either choccy biccies or orange juice would help," Kyra laughed as she opened the bedroom door.

"No scientific reason. You sound like Noah now!" Lauren teased as they trotted down the stairs and Kyra turned and swatted her friend playfully.

The doorbell sounded just as she reached the bottom step and Kyra shrugged in answer to Lauren's questioning look. She wasn't expecting anyone. "Okay, I'll get rid of whoever that is. You get the supplies," she instructed.

As she turned, however, her attention was captured by the dimness of the lounge to her right, usually the brightest room of the house. Pushing open the door, she frowned in confusion as she realised the navy suede curtains had been pulled closed. They'd definitely been open when she and Lauren had come in earlier. Taking a step into the room, she wondered if Liam had come home without them hearing him, but couldn't imagine why he would have closed the curtains.

Instead it was Noah she saw at the far end of the room, huddled over the computer, tapping away fervently on the keyboard. It wasn't unusual for Noah to let himself into their house. He'd spent so much time there over the years that he was practically a member of the family, and even had his own key. It was unusual for him to be there so early, however. More importantly though, she was suddenly panicked that he might have heard what they were doing upstairs. This was, of course, completely irrational as the bedroom door was closed and they hadn't exactly been loud.

"Noah, when did you get here?" she asked and he jumped visibly at her voice. He was so absorbed by what he was doing he hadn't even heard her enter the room. So there was absolutely no way he'd heard what they were talking about upstairs, Kyra noted with relief.

"Ship, Kyra, you scared me." He spun around in the swivel chair to face her, and Kyra smiled at his use of the childhood swear word they'd made up to avoid getting in trouble for using the real thing. "I only got here a few minutes ago. Have loads I need to get done on the website."

"Okay, but why on Earth do you need to do it in complete darkness?" she asked.

"Oh, the light was catching the monitor. Couldn't see a thing," he muttered and turned back to face the screen.

Kyra eyed him suspiciously. She didn't know much about computers, but she did know that light didn't reflect from that kind of flat screen monitor. He was lying and Kyra knew with certainty the real reason he'd closed the curtains. He was hiding, and it didn't take a genius to figure out from whom, which meant things were even more serious than she'd feared. But before she could grill him the doorbell rang out again impatiently.

Kyra didn't miss the way Noah tensed at the sound and glanced at her nervously as she left the room. She saw the fear in his eyes before he broke eye contact and she knew who he expected to be at the door. Pulling the lounge door closed behind her, her way of telling Noah she wouldn't reveal his presence in the house, she stomped down the hallway with determination, feeling not fear in her belly, but anger.

How dare Marco bloody DiCarmello do this to Noah? Who the hell did he think he was? She pulled open the door all ready to let rip, but stopped herself just in time to prevent the stream of obscenities that were poised to burst from her open mouth when she saw that it was Crystal standing in front of her, not Marco.

"Oh...hi."

"Hi, Kyra," Crystal beamed.

"Hi," Kyra repeated and immediately felt like an idiot. Crystal was looking at her expectantly and for a moment she wondered if she had missed something. Was she supposed to be expecting Crystal? Had she invited the girl over and then forgotten? "Can I help you?" she asked.

"Oh, no. But I think maybe I can help you," Crystal replied mysteriously.

"Oka-ay," Kyra said, drawing out the word, trying desperately to work out what the girl was talking about. "What can you help me with?"

"With the Dream Riding of course," she stated.

"The Dream whatying?" Kyra asked, beginning to wonder if Crystal's ice cool exterior was hiding some seriously loose screws.

"Honey, I think we all know what we're talking about. You know, you travel around in an energy body, leaving your physical body behind. Dream Riding."

Now Kyra really did feel stupid. Crystal was talking about the flying, of course. And of course she had seen Kyra the other night. She just hadn't wanted to discuss it in school. Kyra stuttered, lost for words. "The...oh, err, yes... "

"Dream Riding." That is such a cool phrase. I like it!" cried Lauren, who was never lost for words. She'd appeared behind Kyra, balancing a tray teetering with a jug of orange juice, glasses, crisps, and biscuits.

"Well, yes, it seems to be the accepted term for it amongst groups of Dream Riders around the world. I guess because it feels like a kind of dream-like state when you're doing it," Crystal explained.

"Oh My God, there are groups of Dream Riders? And they are all around the world? This is awesome!" Lauren's volume was increasing in tune with her excitement and Kyra shushed her, gesturing toward the lounge and mouthing "Noah."

"You guys have a lot to learn, huh?" Crystal smiled.

"I guess we do," Kyra replied in hushed tones. "So what exactly did you mean when you said you could help me?"

"Well, no offence but it looked like you were struggling with the whole teaching Lauren to Dream Ride thing. I think I can help." Lauren and Kyra both stared at Crystal open-mouthed, both thinking the same thing. How the hell did she know? Given a couple of minutes for the old brain cogs to kick in, the answer was obvious. She'd been in the bedroom, Dream Riding.

"Well I guess you'd better come in and help us eat this junk before it ends up all over the floor," Kyra smiled, motioning to the tray as Lauren yelped with excitement behind her. As Kyra tailed the girls up the stairs, she realised the memory of the boy at the window was still lurking in her mind and she hugged it to herself like a long-loved teddy.

Chapter 18

Just half an hour later, with the use of a surprisingly simple technique called "Buzzy Fingers, Buzzy Feet" (as Lauren had christened it), Crystal had actually achieved the seemingly impossible. Lauren's exhilaration was tangible as she lifted up from her body and floated toward the ceiling. Her excitement radiated from her in waves that pulsed through the room, sweeping the other two girls along on a tide of joy.

"I did it! Oh My God, this is awesome!" Lauren shouted, still the loudest girl in the room even with no voice. "Oh My God, this is weird, but, like, fantastic weird. You look all light and kind of transparent. You both look so beautiful. Everything does. Oh My God, look how everything sparkles!"

She swept around the room in an arc while Kyra and Crystal floated patiently by the window, sharing Lauren's enjoyment of her first Dream Ride, both remembering their own maiden voyages. This was the moment, the amazing moment they'd been dreaming of.

Kyra marvelled at how quickly Lauren took to controlling her movements and wondered if there was anything the girl wasn't excellent at. Of course both other girls heard her thoughts and they all giggled, then giggled even harder when they realised nobody could hear them but themselves.

"Lauren, you think this is good – wait 'til you get out here!" Kyra said and moved backward through the window, feeling the fresh evening breeze. Kyra had no fear of moving through objects now. The first few times there had been an element of doubt, of what if? But now that she felt comfortable in the knowledge that she was safe, she could easily identify how light her energy was. She knew with certainty there was no way she could clash with such a dense physical object while she was travelling in her light body. Only the low vibrations of her physical body could create such a collision and she knew also that she had complete control over when she returned to her physical body. Dream Riding was already second nature.

Kyra slowly moved backward, only taking her eyes off Lauren briefly to glance meaningfully at Crystal, who understood and followed her outside. All eyes were on Lauren. Floating around inside the room was one thing. Having the courage to go against everything that felt natural and hurtle face first at a solid object was another thing entirely. Before Kyra had a chance to start coaxing her best friend out with reassurances, Lauren had zoomed full speed through the window and was half way down the road.

"Is there actually nothing you are scared of?" Crystal enquired with a smile as she and Kyra rode at Lauren's side.

"Actually, don't tell anyone but I'm terrified of clowns. Those creepy white mouths and freakishly big shoes, ugh!" Lauren said it with such seriousness that they couldn't help but laugh again as they drifted along above the rooftops.

Gradually soaring higher and higher, they were soon travelling through the odd puffs of white clouds that were nothing more than mist up close, simple beads of sparkling water. They were heading toward the sea and could already see it up ahead from this high vantage point. They could, of course, have simply thought themselves there but in silent agreement they flew for the sheer pleasure of the journey.

"Oh wow, can you feel that breeze on your face? And the sun on your back? It's like feeling everything that's good, but feeling it a million times more intensely than you ever have before."

"Isn't it just the most amazing feeling? Just perfection," Kyra agreed. "And look at the view from up here, it's stunning." Kyra wondered if it would ever fail to take her breath away.

The sun was beginning to sink in the evening sky, streaking the tops of the clouds with a tinge of pink. And farther below, the houses and streets were spread out like a Lego town, the people hurrying home from work like little scurrying insects. Stepping out of it all and seeing its vastness put a new perspective on the world, on life.

"Just wait until you get over the sea. That is just surreal. You think the air feels amazing, wait until you feel the water. You can dive right into the ocean. It's like some kind of magic rejuvenating potion," Crystal revealed.

"What are we waiting for? Let's go!" Lauren enthused, eager to try everything.

The girls zoomed through the azure sky at a speed not usually possible without the aid of an engine, yet with an effervescence achieved not even by the lightest birds, which afforded them complete lack of resistance. Travelling side by side they set off for their ocean adventure, like a scene from Peter Pan.

Chapter 19

After the incident at the front door, Noah found it hard to concentrate on the website. He'd really thought it was Marco, that the bully had tracked him down to Kyra's house. He was starting to wonder if he'd ever feel safe anywhere. The relief he'd felt when he heard a girl's voice instead was immense. An American girl. Another one of Kyra's new friends it seemed.

For someone who'd been a sworn tomboy for her whole childhood, Kyra had certainly taken a U-turn and become a certified girly-girl since they'd entered their teenage years. It was nice to see her finally feeling more comfortable with herself. He was truly happy for her. And it didn't matter to him how much pink she wore, or how many gooey romance books she read (neither of which she actually did). To him Kyra would always be the kid who could climb higher trees than he could and pick up bigger spiders.

He'd browsed YouTube for a while, trying to distract himself with the latest videos, but even the antics and misdemeanours people caught on camera weren't enough to stop him constantly peering toward the curtains to make sure there were no small gaps through which he was possibly being watched. Eventually he'd given up and wandered through to the kitchen to make himself a snack and satisfy his rumbling tummy. He hadn't hung around at home long enough to eat the food his mum had made, let alone to cook rice to go with it as she had instructed. He'd have to go home before she returned from work to dispose of the evidence. Just thinking about going home alone made him stomach lurch, so he put it out of his mind.

After exploring the cupboards he eventually decided a Dean Koontz novel. He'd read the first page three times before he gave up on that too, realising he wasn't going to be able to concentrate on anything tonight.

He was drumming his fingers against the table, wishing Lauren and the American girl would go home so he could talk to Kyra. His contemplation had led him to a major decision. He really did need to confess all to his best friend before he buckled under the weight of his own fear. He was planning what he would say to her, trying to find the right words, when a loud squeal from upstairs pierced his eardrums. He jumped to his feet in fright, his heart drumming a bass beat in his chest. He was already at the foot of the stairs before he registered that the squeal had been followed by giggles and was therefore probably one of excitement and not terror or pain. He rolled his eyes. Girls.

The raised voices from upstairs were babbling at Olympic speed, but even slowed down he wouldn't have been able to make out the words, muffled as they were by the floor in-between rooms. What on Earth are they doing up there? he wondered as he slowly ascended the stairs, telling himself he needed to visit the loo anyway. The commotion became louder still and it was Lauren's voice out-squealing the rest. No surprise there, he thought as he reached the top landing and walked toward the bathroom, slowing as he passed Kyra's closed bedroom door. There was no need for him to wrestle with his conscience about ear-wigging. From this close proximity the voices were plain to hear without any extra effort.

"Oh My God, I can fly! Kyra, we can do it, we can have great flying adventures together!" Lauren's voice boomed and then she squealed again.

This was quickly followed by a "Shhh" from Kyra and in a quieter voice. "I know. This is amazing. Crystal. I can't believe you did it. You taught Lauren to Dream Ride!"

"It was my pleasure girls, and welcome to the world of Dream Riders!" the American girl replied.

Noah raised his eyebrows and moved closer to the door.

Chapter 20

The second visit to the event that had stolen his sleep the night before with the worry and dread it had conjured was only marginally more helpful than the first, and definitely no more pleasant. Sitting up, the Visitor glanced around to check he was still alone. Not a single person in sight. Only golden wheat could be seen in all directions from his position beneath a large oak tree in between two vast fields.

It was one of his favourite places to come and rest his body during Dream Rides – particularly when he was trying to induce a visit, although they were never guaranteed. He was still trying to work out the key to controlling them.

At least a mile from the nearest road, there was no path between the fields and so this spot afforded him the privacy and tranquillity that were, in his experience, the most important ingredients for a successful Dream Ride. Added to that was his favourite sound: silence. Not complete silence, but a soundtrack completely devoid of human made noise, cars and voices, music, and machines, which was good enough for him.

The soft breeze swished gently through the tall grasses, punctuated only by the occasional cricket and bird song. He shifted backward until he was resting against the trunk of the tree and grabbed the notebook he'd placed carefully beside him when he'd arrived.

When: around a week? Weather: thunderstorm, rain. Location: somewhere high. People: two involved. Possibly both in trouble, or one threatening other?

He still hadn't heard the words. That was the most frustrating thing. This time he'd been closer. He'd just about been able to make out the two figures ahead of him, dark shapes, barely visible against a leaden night sky.

He had no ability to intervene or affect anything during his visits. He could merely observe, and so hadn't been able to get closer for a better look.

He'd had a sense they were up high, near an edge of something with only a low wall between them and a long drop. A streak of lightning in the sky beyond had provided a momentary backlight, making the shapes more defined. One had been pacing, gesturing wildly. The other figure, slightly smaller, had seemed to cower away. And then they'd gone dark again. That was as much as he'd seen before his reality had faded back to the present time, the blue sky and golden wheat, and he'd returned to his physical body immediately to make his notes.

Now that he was back in his body, the emotions attacked him with gusto. He was terrified that if he could stay a bit longer and watch the outcome of the event he'd visited he would witness a tragic death. That was the precise reason why he had to hone his tool and learn to control it, so he could stay longer. Not because he wanted to witness the outcome. The outcome was changeable. One thing he'd learned over the past few months about visiting was that no future event was set in stone. The ability of humans to make choices meant that their possible futures are constantly shifting. No, he needed to learn to make himself stay longer, so he could work out how to get closer and identify the people and places involved. Then he could find them and figure out a way to prevent the event from ever happening. That was his mission now. That was his duty. And he had under a week in which to do it.

Chapter 21

The three girls were sitting cross-legged in a triangle on Kyra's rug. It was the same rug she'd been sitting on the very first time Nana Anna had communicated with her from beyond the grave. She made a mental note that she would NEVER get rid of this rug. It must be some kind of special charm.

Although they didn't know her well, the bond she and Lauren now shared with Crystal was already a strong one. The events of the last hour had cemented their friendship in a way that would have taken months for normal people. Kyra smiled when she realised she now quite liked being able to class herself as something other than "normal." It was amazing how much could change in just a few short days.

"So, Crystal, tell us more about these groups of Dream Riders. Where are they? And what do they do?" she asked. They'd already covered numerous topics of conversation. For example, what Crystal's brother Ray liked to do in his spare time (that one was initiated by Lauren – the answer was basketball, basketball, and more basketball). Then they'd discussed what music Ray liked to listen to (again, initiated by Lauren – the answer to that one was mostly pop, some nu jazz). Next Lauren had started probing about how many girlfriends Ray had had, but Kyra had finally managed to cut her off before Crystal had a chance to answer.

"Well, I have to admit my knowledge is limited, but I've always been inquisitive and tried to learn as much as I can from the Dream Riders I've met. There are groups pretty much everywhere, as far as I know, all over the world."

"Okay, so what are they for – what's the point in them?" Lauren quizzed.

"Apparently they always form to help people in some way or another."

"What do you mean help people? Help how?" Lauren asked in response to Crystal's answer.

"Well, one person I met said groups often form to help keep the world moving in the right direction. I quote: 'Toward peace and happiness.'" Crystal smiled.

"So how do the groups form?" Kyra wondered out loud.

"I'm not really sure exactly how. But it's a question I've asked plenty of times myself. From the stories I've heard it seems people are usually guided together in some way. A few people said they were told by a spirit guide that they should join with certain people. And I've also met people who just followed their instinct. It seems that often people just find themselves in a situation where they come together with others and they know it's meant to be."

"Have you ever been in a Dream Riding group?" Lauren asked.

"I never have...until now."

"You mean...us, we, we are a group? A group of, you know, Dream Riders?" Lauren's eyes lit up and Kyra had to admit to feeling a jolt of excitement herself.

"Well, when I saw Kyra at the school last night I knew it wasn't an accident. Something had told me to travel there, right at that moment. I was actually really excited. At last I was feeling that gut instinct I'd heard about from others so many times. Why were you there Kyra?"

Kyra thought back for a moment. "Well, actually, somebody kind of suggested it."

"You mind telling me who?"

"Well...my Nana Anna... "

84

"Kyra, I hope you don't mind me asking this but is your Nana Anna in the spirit world?"

"I don't mind you asking, of course not. And yes, she is," Kyra replied, slightly bemused.

"I thought so. And does she come and talk to you, you know, help you out when you need help?" Crystal continued her line of questioning.

Kyra didn't need to even answer that one. She just nodded in agreement.

"I met a man in Canada once who'd had a Native American Chief visiting him every morning since he was eleven years old, giving him advice about the day ahead. He told me this man was his spirit guide. Kyra, I may be wrong, but I think your Nana Anna is your spirit guide. If so, I would guess she suggested you fly to the school for a reason – the most likely reason being for us to meet." Crystal was up on her knees now, leaning close to the other girls, her eyes wide with excitement. "And your instinct told you that teaching Lauren to Dream Ride was the right thing to do, right?" Kyra nodded again although Crystal obviously didn't need the confirmation. She was on a roll. "Well one thing I've definitely learned over the years is that there is nothing we can rely on more strongly than our own instinct. I really think all this means that we were guided together, drawn together. We ARE a Dream Riding group already." She punctuated this last point by slapping her knees.

"Oh my God. Oh my God. Oh my God. This is amazing. So we, like, what do we do now? T-shirts, we need T-shirts, you know, to show that we're part of a group. T-shirts with our names on the back, and our logo on the front." Lauren was absolutely brimming with excitement, her blue eyes wide, her hands flapping. Kyra and Crystal both turned and looked at her, their expressions identical, amused exasperation.

"Okay, okay," Lauren said and held her hands up to fend off their glares.

Kyra rolled her eyes. "I think we should just go with the flow, take each day at a time and listen to our instinct. Let's just enjoy it!"

The girls all grinned at each other and then Crystal closed her eyes and took a deep breath, resting her hands on her legs. Kyra wondered if she was praying or something. Catching sight of the clock on her bedside table she realised it must be getting close to dinner time and she was ravenous. Pizza is definitely on the menu tonight as soon as dad gets home!

"Oooh yummy, chicken and bacon and extra pepperoni on mine please!" Crystal said opening her eyes and flashing a mischievous smile.

"What? How?" Kyra began, stumped. "You knew what I was thinking?"

Crystal giggled. "Sorry I couldn't help myself, honey. Showing you was the easiest way to explain. Well, and kind of fun too! Since we're sharing all the weird and wonderful things we can do, we might as well cover everything. Yes, I can read people's thoughts while I'm Dream Riding. You know the way we communicate in thought when we're riding, right?" Both girls nodded, they had gotten used to that pretty quickly. "Well we can choose which thoughts we send out to each other. Pretty much like talking, we choose what we say. But I seem to be able to read all the thoughts of everyone, even people who are not Riding."

"Oh my God, wow. So you can like, just read what everyone is thinking all the time?"

"Well, I have to be Riding. If I'm in my body I can't do it, I don't know why. But it's simple enough. I've been riding for so long now I can just nip in and out of my body as easy as snapping my fingers. So if I want to know what someone is thinking, I just close my eyes and hover on out for a second."

"How does that work? Do you hear their thoughts?" Kyra asked.

"Well, I see kind of pictures, sometimes images of the words a person is thinking, sometimes a vision of what they can see in their mind."

"That's amazing. I'm going to have to watch what I'm thinking now, though!" Lauren laughed.

"Yes, especially about my brother," Crystal joked. They all

laughed.

"How long have you actually been Dream Riding?" Lauren enquired. And Kyra realised that despite the amount of talking Crystal had done, they still knew very little about her.

"Since I was seven," she answered, jumping to her feet. "Now, I'm starving. Did somebody mention pizza?"

Glancing again at the clock Kyra noted it was five on the dot. Her father and brother would be walking through the door any moment. So they should be safe to order pizza in the knowledge that somebody with a wallet would be home by the time it arrived. "Okay, I'm gonna let you get away with that subject change for now, but only because my stomach is growling like an angry dog. After food, the focus is on Crystal Hudson," Kyra said with a grin, only half joking, as she stood up.

"Yes, we want details!" Lauren added, jumping to her feet and stretching her arms up high.

"Okay, okay," Crystal laughed and held her hands up as if in surrender. "I'll tell you everything."

Something suddenly occurred to Kyra. "Hey, Crystal, Lauren's sleeping over tonight. Wanna join us and make it a slumber party?" She glanced at Lauren to make sure that was okay with her and Lauren's wide smile told her it was.

"Well sure, that would be great. Midnight Dream Riding, yay! I'll call my Mom but I'm sure it will be fine."

"Fantastic, this will be so cool!" Kyra moved toward the door and grasped the handle, pulling it open. She nearly jumped right out of her skin when she found Noah standing directly in front of her. He leapt backward.

"Kyra, I, uh, I was just,...err,...just,...err. I was making a drink and thought I'd see if you girls wanted anything," he stuttered, looking down awkwardly.

Kyra frowned at him, confused, but he avoided her gaze. "We were actually just coming down to order some pizza. Want to join us?" she asked, trying to act normally.

"Sure," he replied and followed her toward the stairs.

Kyra's brain was ticking over. Why had Noah been listening at her door? It didn't seem like Noah at all, and more importantly, how much had he heard?

Chapter 22

It had seemed such a simple task when Lauren had suggested it yesterday morning: "Decide where you would go for half an hour if you were invisible and distance was no object."

They'd all awakened tired but happy after their late night DVD, and even later night Dream Ride. Before going their separate ways for the weekend, Lauren had insisted they have official meetings for their Cranley Dream Riding Group. All had been in agreement after much badgering from Lauren, and Kyra had to admit it sounded like fun. The only problem was deciding what they would actually do. Sitting around and waiting for the reason they'd come together to make itself apparent was not an option where Miss Lockett was concerned. And so they'd eventually decided that for their first meeting on Monday, they would allow themselves to play a bit and get in some Dream Riding practice at the same time. Surely it was everyone's dream to have the power of invisibility? Well they had it, and so they'd agreed that over the weekend they would all decide on a mini adventure they could go on. They'd made a pact to participate in each other's adventures, no matter what they may be.

Ok think, Kyra instructed herself, *you can come up with something good. What's the one thing you always wanted to do?* She began writing a mental list.

Manchester United locker room. Definitely a top choice. She was excited for a moment, but then realised it was out of season and there would be nobody there on a Monday evening at this time of year. She thought and thought, but that was it. She drew a complete blank. That was literally all she could think of. Pathetic.

Sliding her butt around easily on the white leather, Kyra sighed and swung her legs over the arm of the sofa, lying on her back and gazing up at the huge skylight for inspiration. Fat drops of rain drummed loudly against the glass, blurring the heavy grey clouds that hung lazily in the sky above. No inspiration there. The clouds had had the cheek to appear just as she'd arrived at her mum's the previous day, and they'd stubbornly grown heavier and darker with each passing hour, pelting down a relentless torrent for over twenty four hours now.

Not that she minded rain. Sometimes it was her favourite type of weather, especially when accompanied by thunder and lightning; she loved the atmosphere of excitement and adventure a storm created. However, when visiting her mum for the weekend, wet weather excluded some of the more fun and frivolous activities she'd become accustomed to as atonement for her mother and soon-to-be stepfather's guilty consciences. High budget shopping sprees, boating on the lake in Wood Vale Park, and arcade games on the pier were just a few examples. Instead she'd spent nearly two days cooped up in a small, although rather luxurious flat, with two of the people who annoyed her most in the world, her brother and Mr. Dupére. Even her mum began to drive her mad after a certain amount of time in a confined space.

For the millionth time that day Kyra found herself slipping easily into a daydream about the boy at the window. She could still picture his face as if he were standing right in front of her, his square jaw, his perfectly shaped mouth, and wide nose. She longed to reach out and touch him, to stroke his silky hair, to feel his warm breathe on her face. Again she asked herself who is he? and fantasised about ways in which she could find him. Not allowing the possibility that she might never see him again to settle in her head, she flicked away the thought with annoyance whenever it fluttered by.

Dupére interrupted her pondering. "Right, the board's all set up, Ky. Come on over. I'm making chocolate milkshakes for you kids. Whipped cream on top?"

Kyra cringed inwardly. Honestly, sometimes she wondered if he thought she was five years old. It must be even worse for her brother, who at eighteen was only seven years younger than Dupére.

Before replying, she reminded herself to make an effort. "Just coming, no cream thanks." she called, pulling herself up and stretching before moving toward the dining area of the open plan flat, where a Monopoly board awaited. Liam pulled a face behind Dupére's back as Kyra sat down, and she tried desperately to suppress a giggle. Instead it escaped as a snort, which she rapidly disguised as a coughing fit, drawing alarmed gazes from her mum and Dupére.

"Are you okay?" he asked, his face scrunched in concern. He decided to thump her repeatedly on the back, despite the vigorous nodding of her head to indicate that she was fine. The back slapping led to another burst of giggles, which in turn set Liam off.

Dupére's confused expression morphed into a smile as he went back to dishing out piles of Monopoly money. "Well I guess I missed the joke, but at least everyone's happy."

This only caused them to laugh even harder at his sheer desperation to please them. A sharp look from their mother sitting like a queen at the head of the table sipping a glass of pink wine finally subdued their laughter. She might be many things but she wasn't stupid. She was quite aware that her children were making fun of her boyfriend. As they began the game, Kyra and her brother shared a secret smile. Maybe he's not as annoying as all that, she thought as she rolled the dice.

As was customary, the game stretched on for hours. At least with the newest version of the board there were rules that allowed for faster play. And by seven that evening it was finally drawing to a close, even after a long break while Dupére had served up the roast dinner. Kyra was close to winning and her task for tomorrow's meeting had been shoved to the back of her mind.

Each and every member of the Sutton family had a competitive streak. Board games were extremely serious business. The first time Dupére had challenged them all to a game of scrabble had been a severe learning curve for him. He'd been loudly shushed a number of times when he'd tried to make conversation during other people's moves. And Kyra's mother had sulked for the remainder of the evening when he'd won the game by fifty points clear. Eventually he'd retreated to the bedroom ashen faced.

He'd obviously re-thought his strategy as now he seemed to be putting no effort in at all, apparently having decided that losing would make for an easier life. And instead of attempting to make conversation, he just smiled inanely the whole time, thoroughly enjoying this family time together, despite the slightly menacing looks of determination on the faces of his fiancé and her offspring.

What a weirdo Kyra thought, not for the first time as she counted out her moves. One, two, three, four...The Natural History Museum. "I'm buying!" she declared, thrilled to finally have the last in the orange set. Now she would be able to finish them all off! As she was counting out her money, something niggled the back of her mind.

Of course – The Natural History Museum! That was the answer. Where would you go for half an hour if you were invisible and distance was no object? With Manchester United ruled out as an option, The Natural History Museum in London after closing hours was definitely her next best choice. A school visit three years ago had sparked an obsession with dinosaurs, and she'd returned a year later after pestering her parents for months until they'd finally given in.

She'd found it even more fascinating than her first visit. With so many displays and collections to explore it would be impossible to ever get bored. She'd always wondered what it would be like there at night time, roaming amongst the huge beasts, and she'd watched the "Night at the Museum" DVDs like a million times over.

Ecstatic to have made her choice, Kyra went back to winning the game with a huge grin lighting up her face.

"You got a message...yeah baby," declared her phone in Austen Power's voice as she passed the dice to Liam.

Need 2 c u tonight

It was Noah's number. Maybe he's finally ready to talk.

Back by 8, I'll come 'round she typed back, as Liam moodily dumped his money and properties back in the bank, declaring surrender.

Chapter 23

He was full of nerves, but for a change it was excited nerves instead of terrified nerves. Ever since Friday evening he'd been wrestling with the decision – should he take the safe option, carry on as normal and pretend he knew nothing? Or should he 'fess up and risk not only humiliation but also losing his best friend, for a chance, just a chance...

In the end he'd decided it was all too much of a coincidence. He couldn't not take the opportunity, and hell, for the first time in weeks, maybe even months, he'd actually spent an entire day and night with barely a fleeting thought of Marco. That was a miracle. Last night had been the best night's sleep he couldn't remember having in donkey's years – actually, never mind donkeys – in elephant's years! So as he pulled open the door to Kyra on Sunday evening he was resolute in his decision.

She offered a smile but no questions. Noah knew the tactic well. She probably thought he'd decided to "open up" about his problem with Marco, in which case she'd say as little as possible in the hope he would spill before changing his mind. Standing back, he let her enter, and after closing the door he motioned for her to follow him up the narrow staircase.

"It's easier to show you, than to try and explain," he said in answer to her questioning expression. The house was exactly the same layout as Kyra's, but mirrored, and Noah's bedroom reflected Kyra's in position – although in no other way whatsoever. Kyra's abode was soft and light, full of colour and character, with pine furniture, a double bed scattered with beaded cushions, and a huge array of fantasy posters adorning the walls, fairies and mermaids, unicorns and magicians. Nothing matched, but like Kyra herself, the eclectic mix was bursting with personality and worked perfectly.

Noah's room was far starker in design with pale blue walls sporting no decoration, a single bed with a faded spaceship quilt cover, and a mismatching wardrobe and desk. The desk itself was dominated by all manner of computer equipment, although most of it was the chunky, old fashioned variety his mum had purchased years ago from a second hand store, instead of the sleeker more expensive machines available nowadays. Unlike most teenage boys' bedrooms, it was spotless, and could only be described as functional. Just the way Noah liked it.

Instead of entering his own room, however, Noah continued to the smaller room at the end of the hallway, the room which was the reflection of Liam's next door. Kyra had only been in Noah's bedroom a handful of times due to the fact he was nearly always at her house, rather than she at his. This third bedroom, she realised, she had never entered. Noah swung open the door and walked into the small space, and Kyra followed, scanning the room, intrigued. Opposite the door was a small window below which was stacked a pile of boxes balancing on a large brown leather suitcase. The walls on either side of her were both covered with floor to ceiling bookshelves, over laden with books, so full they were actually overflowing, some of the books even spilling out onto the floor. The room contained no other furniture at all.

It wasn't what Kyra had expected to see in here. For some reason she'd always assumed it was a spare bedroom. Being a complete bookworm for, like, her whole life, she was oddly excited at the sheer amount of them, hardbacks and paperbacks, in all shapes and sizes, their spines boasting all manner of typefaces and colours. Moving closer to one of the shelves on her right she peered at random covers, scanning their titles.

Beyond Death by Lucas Pomsford, Projectiology by Waldo Vierra, The Celestine Prophecy by James Redfield. The list went on and on, each title more intriguing than the last. Turning to Noah, who was watching her silently, she said, "Okay, they're books. They're weird sounding books. Feel free to explain any time, won't you?" She was only half joking.

Lifting one of the smaller boxes from the top of the pile, Noah plonked himself down on the floor leaning back against a larger box and patted a space beside him. Once Kyra was seated he rifled through the box until he'd found what he was seeking, a small red photo album. Opening it to the first page he silently handed it to Kyra.

"Your dad... " she stated quietly, gazing down at a smiling bride and groom. The bride was unmistakably Noah's mum. The groom was recognisable as his father, not only from the framed photograph in the lounge that had become so familiar over the years she'd stopped really looking at it, but also from the remarkable similarity to Noah himself. Kyra was shocked by the likeness between father and son, so obvious now that Noah was just a few years younger than his father had been when the photo was taken. Studying the picture more closely she could see Mr. Pinkerton had the same thick black hair as his son, curling stubbornly in all directions, giving the effect that it had never seen a brush. There was also an amazing likeness in the squarish set of the chin and the lopsided kink in the bridge of his nose. The most striking resemblance, however, was the piercing directness of his milk chocolate eyes.

Glancing over at the pile of boxes, she guessed they probably all contained stuff belonging to his father, maybe the suitcase too. All these years after her husband's death, Noah's mother still hadn't been able to let go of his things. Noah had rarely talked to her about his dad, and she'd never asked. Why was he showing her a picture of him now? Puzzled, she waited for the explanation she sensed was imminent. He looked up and held her gaze as he spoke, "It's a skill, Kyra. I've known about it for ages...and I know that anyone who tries hard enough can do it. I've wanted to do it for so long... "

Kyra was stumped, ideas running through her head. Some little part of her inside knew what he meant but she couldn't quite grasp how he could be talking about that. "I don't understand. What's a skill? What's that got to do with your dad?" she stuttered lamely, her thoughts still refusing to form any kind of cohesive or useful response.

He maintained eye contact for a moment more, and she could tell he was trying to decide if she was humouring him or if he really hadn't made himself clear enough. Picking up the album, he focussed on the picture of his parents and said, with a voice that seemingly came from a more distant place, "My mum and I have spent a long time learning all about the afterlife. It's a real passion for her. It's what kept her going back then, and seeking more information - it's become a way of life for me." He paused for a long time, so long that Kyra wondered if he was expecting a response. Just as she opened her mouth to speak, he continued, "But there's so much more to it than just death. Every time I pick up a book I learn something new. Like what you can do, for example."

There was no doubt this time. He was obviously talking about Dream Riding.

"You heard?" she asked, but the answer was obvious. A vision filled her head of him scurrying along the hallway as she'd emerged from her bedroom on Friday, so obviously guilty of ear wigging. He'd overheard everything they'd discussed. He didn't answer but nodded slowly in affirmation and continued to explain himself.

"Since two years after my father died, my mother has been going to spiritualist churches hoping to get a message from him. She's heard nothing yet..."

"Spiritualist churches?" Kyra queried, her mind choosing to nitpick at the details instead of deal with the overall weirdness of the situation.

"It's like a church, but instead of a vicar or priest a medium talks to the congregation." In response to Kyra's blank expression he added, "A medium is somebody who can talk to spirits. They give out messages to people, messages from their loved ones who've died."

She'd no idea such places existed, and wondered how many more revelations there would be tonight. Noah continued, "Anyway, since I was nine, I've been doing my own research and reading, discovering different ways people can contact those in the afterlife." He lifted his eyes and met her gaze once more. "Some Dream Riders can do it, if they have the gift."

This one really did take her by surprise. Her mouth opened, trying to form words, but failing. Eventually she managed, "You think I can contact your dad?" she gaped, still struggling to comprehend what he was saying.

"No," he responded. "I think I can. With your help, that is."

The whole conversation seemed surreal. She was having trouble getting a grip on it. Here was Mr. Facts and Figures coming out with the weirdest stuff she could imagine. And she'd always been so sure he wouldn't believe in anything that wasn't solid or couldn't be proven. It was unbelievable. Noah had spent years trying to contact the afterlife and she'd spent years trying to hide the fact that she could.

"But hold on a second. You don't believe in anything. I mean, there's no formula here, there are no calculations, no science. What are you doing even thinking about this stuff? It's just so not you!" she frowned. It was crazy, almost as if he was making it up. Was he taking the Mickey out of her?

He stood up, strode to a bookshelf, and ran his finger along a row of books near the top. "According to many of the books in this section, it is a science. It's called Astral Projection, the ability to have controlled out of body experiences. It has been proven over and over in experiments, and has been common practice in many cultures throughout the world for millennia. As has communicating with the spirits of deceased loved ones. Many believe that the two practices are linked. And you're the living proof." He paused before adding, "I want to be too."

She was almost speechless. Okay, so the books proved he wasn't teasing her, and anyway, she knew really that Noah wouldn't do that. But how could she not have known about his obsession? She lay back on the carpet, stared up at the ceiling and said, "Why did you never tell me? You knew all this stuff. It's been such a huge part of your life. How could you hide it from me?"

"I could ask you the same question," he replied with a mischievous smile and a twinkle in his eye. She returned the grin despite herself as he continued, "But right now I'm too happy. I've read so many times on various forums that if it's your destiny to be a Dream Rider the right situation will present itself, at the right time. And now it has, Kyra, don't you see?" He stood up again and while walking around the room gestured toward the heavens with his hands, almost as if he'd had a massive revelation. "You see, Kyra, according to some texts, all people are intrinsically linked. And on a global level... "

"Oh, come on now, Noah," she interrupted. "You can't possibly manage to turn this into one of your boring science lessons! I knew Nerd Noah was still in there somewhere."

They looked at each other for a second and the expression of deep concentration on his face broke into a wide grin. They started laughing hysterically. It was the kind of laugh that carried on and on, an almost manic laugh born of relief and excitement. The small room was filled with not only with their jubilant laughter, but also the magical anticipation of all that was to come.

Chapter 24

"Oh My God, I still can't believe it. I mean, Noah of all people, he's just so, so, so...Noah!" Lauren exclaimed again.

Kyra sat on her bed, hands in her lap, eyebrows raised. She'd been unsure how her friend would react to the news and her reaction had, in fact, been pretty similar to Kyra's own. Utter disbelief. "It's odd, isn't it? He's known about Dream Riding all this time. In fact, he knows way more about it than we do – theoretically, at least," she replied.

"I guess there really is no knowing what's in that funny little head of his," Lauren said with a smile. And Kyra was surprised to find herself feeling quite defensive on her friend's behalf, even though she could tell Lauren meant it jokingly. He may seem odd to people who didn't know him well, but he was harmless. And after their talk last night she felt closer to him than she had in a long time.

"He's not that odd. He's just more reserved than most people. And he's, like, really clever. People in this world seem to hate people who are cleverer than they are," Kyra said, ignoring Lauren's raised eyebrows. "And he's really serious about this. He's belonged to these secret online forums for years, trying to find ways of learning to do it," she said, as if stating his case in a court of law.

"It is kind of a coincidence isn't it? Here we are, Riding away without even knowing the proper name for it, and there's Science

Boy, desperate to do it!" Lauren smiled. Kyra gritted her teeth. Lauren just wasn't getting her point. Did she have to spell it out? Lauren resumed her pacing of the bedroom, purple summer dress shimmying around her as she moved back and forth, back and forth, silver gladiator sandals marking a path in the newly vacuumed shaggy carpet.

Looking down Kyra realised she was underdressed in comparison, in her charcoal grey leggings and black rock chick T-shirt, with only neon pink slippers to liven up the outfit. Nothing new there. Although she'd started making a bit more of an effort with her clothes since befriending Lauren, right now she didn't really care. She had a more important matter to focus on: her promise to Noah.

"I wondered, well, hoped really, that maybe we could try to teach him. I wanted to bring him today, but thought I'd better ask permission from you guys first – since we're all members of the club, and have to make decisions together and all. I guess it might change the dynamic of the group a bit. I mean I know him of course, but it could be weird for you and Crystal," Kyra rambled. She hoped beyond hope the others would agree to let him in.

"Hmm...I know what you mean. He's – well he's nice – but he's not the easiest person in the world to be around. He's a little... intense." Lauren studied her baby pink nail varnish as she walked, not realising what a blow her words were. How could Kyra tell Noah he couldn't join the club? He'd be devastated. Before she could protest, Lauren continued, "But then you guys did teach me to do it, so I suppose it wouldn't be fair to not give him that same chance. Maybe we should wait 'til Crystal gets here and see what she thinks. You know, make a group decision."

Kyra's hopes lifted marginally, but she was still disappointed. Lauren wasn't exactly jumping with joy to welcome a new member into the group, and Kyra had hoped to get her friend's backup before tackling Crystal. At least it wasn't a "no." And it was only fair that they make all decisions affecting the group together, democratically. "Okay," she agreed.

Still pacing, Lauren reached the window and peeked out for the gazillionth time. "Do you think she'll be here soon?" she asked, turning toward Kyra. She obviously didn't expect an answer as she continued nattering. "Oh, pipsqueak, did I bring all the supplies?" Rushing to the desk where she'd laid out her tools for the meeting ahead, she scanned the items, an A-4 ring binder with "Cranley Dream Riding Group – Confidential" emblazoned across the front, three small notebooks, one for each of them, with their names doodled prettily on the cover, heaps of stationary and a pile of plain paper, for God knows what, thought Kyra as she watched her friend with amusement. Lauren's bubbly energy was, as always, infectious.

Ding-dong, the doorbell sang. Lauren jumped and did an excited jig, hopping from foot to foot and flapping her hands in the air. They raced down the stairs. Kyra was still buzzing about Noah's revelations and eager to find out if he could join the group.

"Hi, Crystal," Lauren enthused with a huge smile as Kyra opened the door. "Oh!" she exclaimed in surprise when she noticed the figure half hidden behind Crystal. Gathering herself, she slipped subtly into cool and sophisticated mode and added, in what Kyra suspected was supposed to be a flirty voice, "Hello, Ray."

"Hey," he said with just a hint of a smile, barely looking up.

Kyra imagined she could hear Lauren's heart speeding up at the sound of his low tone and had to bite her cheek to keep from laughing.

"Hi Crystal, Ray." Kyra stood back to let them in, her expression smiling but questioning, waiting for Crystal to explain the presence of her brother.

"Hi guys. Listen – I didn't want to say anything until I'd had a chance to talk to Ray, but I think he's meant to be a part of the group. We talked and he agreed to come along today and see if he feels the same."

"You mean, he Dream Rides?" Lauren asked, her voice suddenly back in excited schoolgirl mode. "Sorry, Ray, I mean you...you can Dream Ride?" He nodded confirmation, head still down. "Oh My God – of course, you're twins, why didn't I think of that? That's so cool!"

Kyra was seething. She'd had the decency to ask permission from the group before introducing a new member, leaving Noah sitting at home by the phone, nervously awaiting their decision, and Crystal just waltzed in here with her brother, assuming he could join, no questions asked. The cheek of it!

"Well actually, Crystal, we were just talking upstairs and we decided that any potential new members need to be app..."

"Ray, it would be an honour for you to join, welcome to the club, come on up," Lauren interrupted. Kyra was left open mouthed. Lauren had kicked up a fuss about Kyra's suggestion to let Noah in, and here she was bending her own rules just because she was going weak at the knees over some lad, like a dippy girl. Kyra was livid.

"Go on up, I'll back in a mo," she called to the three figures trooping up the stairs, her surprisingly calm voice not betraying any of the anger she felt. To hell with asking permission, let's all just do whatever the flip we want. Throwing the front door open with force, she marched across the front lawn and hopped over the small dividing fence between their front garden and next doors. Noah answered about a millisecond after her first knock.

"Ky, I thought you were going to phone?" he frowned in confusion and held up the mobile in his hand, where it had been clenched for the past hour as he eagerly awaited the decision. "What happened? Did they agree?"

"Screw them! It seems we don't operate democratically after all. Come on, let's go." She grabbed his arm and practically dragged him across the two front gardens and up the stairs into her bedroom, where three faces looked up quizzically.

"Let me introduce Noah, the newest member of our group," she announced with a smug smile on her face. If others could just barge in with new people, then so could she. Let's see how they like that!

"Well, hi, Noah. Nice to meet you. I'm Crystal," Crystal said as she stood and offered her hand. Noah shook it awkwardly.

"Hi, Crystal. Nice to meet you," he muttered. Ray gave his

customary nod and half smile which Noah mirrored in return, and Lauren resumed twirling a strand of hair around her finger and making doe eyes at Ray, who couldn't possibly have noticed as he was looking nowhere but down at his (astonishingly huge) trainers.

"Kyra, I'm sorry for offending you by bringing Ray without asking. I really didn't think you'd mind after all that stuff we talked about the other day, about being guided and stuff. But I'm sorry, I should have asked first." Crystal smiled sheepishly. "And I'm really happy for Noah to be here. If you feel he's meant to be here and he feels he's meant to be here, then that's good enough for me; he's obviously meant to be here."

Kyra was dumbstruck for a moment, but then realisation dawned on her...Crystal had read her mind...and while she was having a major strop too. The last of the anger dissolved from her body and she felt a flush of embarrassment colour her cheeks. "Oh, God, I'm sorry. I acted like such a baby." Why was she so impulsive? Crystal was so calm, so nice. And she made so much sense.

"Honey, don't be embarrassed. It's okay. This is new for all of us." Kyra smiled gratefully and then her eyes met Lauren's. Her friend gave her a supportive smile, and Kyra immediately felt like a complete bitch. She smiled back.

"Okay," Lauren said in an authoritative tone, hopping up from her position on the bed. "Well I hadn't banked on there being so many of us, but I do have spares. So we should be able to make do. Okay, you three sit there," she instructed, motioning toward the bed. "And you can stay there, that's fine," she added to Ray, who was already seated in the desk chair. Leaning over him she scooped up the pile of notebooks and handed one to each person, quickly scribbling the names of the new members on the front of their books. After retrieving the large folder, she positioned herself on the floor, her back against the wardrobe, and opened it up to the first blank sheet of paper.

"Welcome, everyone, to the first meeting of the Cranley Dream Riders Group!" she announced. "What you have in your hand is your personal journal – to keep track of everything that happens at all times, during and in-between meetings. You can write events, thoughts, feelings, whatever you like. You don't have to share the contents of your diary, but will be given the opportunity at every meeting should you wish to do so." She paused and smiled before continuing. "I think it's very important to keep these notes as we don't yet know the purpose of our group and we may at some point need to look back on events and piece the clues together."

Kyra smiled inwardly. Lauren was in her element. And she was so funny too. How could Kyra have ever been mad at her?

"The first item on the agenda is... " Lauren looked up with a very serious expression on her face.

"...teaching Noah to Dream Ride!" the three girls said in unison.

Chapter 25

"Something's holding you back. I think your conscious mind *thinks* you want to do it, but some part of your subconscious doesn't agree." Crystal looked kindly at Noah, seated beside her on the floor. He avoided her gaze by fiddling with a strand of the rug between his fingers. None of them needed to be a mind reader to read between the lines; she thought he was scared. Kyra ached for him, knowing how badly he wanted this. Was it true – was he scared of succeeding, and possibly eventually meeting his father? She wondered briefly if all the technical knowledge he'd amassed in his years of research was going to actually be any help at all, and she guessed by the look on his face that he was wondering the same thing.

"Buzzy Fingers, Buzzy Feet," "The Rollover," and "The Step Up." He'd tried them all. The first two were Crystal's sworn techniques for Dream Riding, the latter being Ray's preferred method. None had worked. Although unlike Lauren when she was learning, Noah had remained calm and patient.

"I just need a break. We've been trying for over an hour now. Anyway, I didn't want to dominate the whole meeting. You guys get on with whatever you were going to do before I barged in. We can try again another time."

He hopped up and seated himself firmly in the desk chair to avoid any protestations, and Kyra could see that he was embarrassed at his inability to leave his physical body despite the willingness of everybody in the group to assist. He'd put a brave smile on his face, but she could see straight through him. She didn't want them to give up on him already – although she wondered if he would feel more comfortable practising alone, now that he had the techniques to try.

"Now how about I stay here while you guys ride?" Noah suggested. "That way if anybody comes upstairs or knocks on the door while you're away, I can distract them until you come back to the physical."

"Oh Noah, that's hardly fair on you. You didn't join the group to act as a guard dog... " Kyra began.

"It's not like that, honestly, Ky. I'm so chuffed just to be a part of all this. It's a relief to finally be around people who understand the realities of life. *All* of life, not just the physical. You don't know how exciting this is for me." He looked sheepish, but it was obvious he meant every word. She too knew how it felt to belong for the first time.

Despite the mix of personalities, they all seemed to mesh, and the banter between them had been fun. Yet at the same time they were all focussed on a common purpose, learning more about every aspect of Dream Riding and discovering why they'd been drawn together. Kyra wondered if Noah was hoping to make himself useful so they would continue to let him hang around whether or not he could actually participate in the rides. She wanted to tell him it wasn't necessary, that he was already a part of the group. But she didn't want to embarrass him further in front of the others.

"Well, when you put it like that...if you're sure... " she said.

"Absolutely. Anyway, I can do some more research online," he said, motioning toward Kyra's computer in front of him. "And I can jot some stuff in my diary." He held up the notebook in his hand, and smiled at Lauren who beamed in return.

"I think it's a fantastic idea! That way we can have our adventures without worrying about someone walking in and finding us all lying around like rag dolls," Lauren said.

"Nice one man," was Ray's contribution to the conversation. In contrast to his sister, he spoke only rarely; and when he did have something to say, he used his words sparingly.

"Thank you, Noah, for the kind offer," Crystal added. "While we're on the subject of our physical bodies, you know, when I'm riding I've always feel like I'm still somehow aware of what's happening in the physical dimension. I know through experience if somebody walks into the room where my physical body is while I'm away riding, I just *know*. I don't know how, but I do. And I return to my body in an instant. Then I just pretend like I was having a nap or something." Everybody smiled at the thought. "Of course, it might look a bit odd if someone entered and we were all just lying flat on our backs on the floor. And so it will definitely be beneficial to have you here, Noah, to distract any visitors long enough for us to get back and look natural!"

"Thanks, Crystal, and I know exactly what you're talking about when you describe physical awareness while Dream Riding." Noah looked excited. "I think I can explain the phenomena. You see our physical bodies and our energy bodies run in parallel. Our physical bodies are merely a mirror image of our energy bodies but made of matter. So anything that happens in or around our physical bodies is instantly 'known' by our energy bodies too. Think of it as an invisible cord that keeps the two bodies attached no matter where they are."

"Okay, Einstein, I think I actually understood some of that!" Lauren joked.

"Wow, dude, that's awesome." Ray actually looked up and smiled, obviously impressed with Noah's knowledge.

"That makes complete sense," Crystal agreed. "Thanks for explaining so clearly."

Kyra felt like a proud mother. She was so pleased Noah was a hit with the rest of the group. "Oh, Noah knows loads of stuff," she bragged.

Noah seemed to have actually forgotten to be nervous and was becoming relaxed with the group. "Well I'm glad to have something to contribute, even if it is only theoretical!"

"We're all here for a reason, and we all bring our own gifts. Yours is no less valid or less useful than anyone else's," said Crystal. "With knowledge like that, you will definitely have more than your fair share to offer to the group!"

Noah looked immensely pleased with himself, his face stretching into a wide smile. "Thank you, Crystal."

Kyra realised she hadn't seen him smile nearly enough recently. It made a nice change.

"Okay, this is getting way too soppy. That's enough of the science bit and enough of the sentimental bit. Let's get this party started!" Lauren called, eager to move the meeting forward. She was flapping her hands again as she jumped to her feet. "Time for some Dream Riding. I hope you all did your homework! Who's going first? Not me, I want to save mine for last. Oh, just so you know what I'm talking about...," she looked from Ray to Noah and back again. "We set ourselves a task over the weekend to think of where we would like to Ride to. We had to all think about where we would choose to go for half an hour if we were invisible and distance was no object. Because of course we are, and it isn't," she explained.

"Well, Ray and I have done this like a trillion times. So we've pretty much seen everything we want to see. You guys should definitely go first before we run out of time," Crystal insisted in a firm tone.

"Okay it's settled. Kyra, you're going first!" Lauren instructed. "And don't worry. There will be no laughing and no questioning each other's choices!" She flashed a warning glare around the room. "So out with it, Ky, where are we going on our first adventure?"

Kyra opened her mouth to protest, but then thought *what the hell?* "Well, okay. Our first destination of the evening will be The Natural History Museum in London," she announced.

Chapter 26

The four Dream Riders hurtled through the glowing mist of multi-coloured energy that was, according to Noah, a time-tunnel, the very substance of everything that would stand between a Dream Rider and its destination in the physical dimension, compacted into just a fraction of a second when said Dream Rider "transports him or herself instantaneously to an alternative physical location." Kyra could just about get her head around that bit, but hadn't even pretended to understand what he was rabbiting on about when he'd expanded into an explanation of how time is just an illusion and we are, in fact, everywhere all at once. Even Crystal, who obviously had a brain for science and a determination to understand everything, had given up trying to get it after his fourth attempt at an explanation.

Emerging from the time tunnel, with its increasingly familiar points of light still twinkling around them like a million stars, the group found themselves face to face with a huge diplodocus. Well, a life-size replica of one at least. Kyra gasped in awe, struck as always by the imposing grandness of the Museum's enormous Central Hall. Swirling full circle she took in the tremendous ceiling overhead with its arched windows lending a clear view of the darkening evening sky, the depth and radiance of the blues amplified by her enhanced senses.

"Wow, this is amazing." The same thought was echoed by all as they took in the sheer expanse of the room and the clear view they had of this main exhibit. Kyra had never before had the opportunity to really see the artefacts in the museum, at least not without being jostled along by hundreds of other visitors, all in a rush to get to the next thing to see, blocking her view and stepping on her toes. She circled the huge dinosaur skeleton slowly, taking in the thickness of the bones, the length of the neck, the sturdy legs.

"Help, help, I've been eaten!" came a cry. And turning her attention back to the others, Kyra couldn't help but laugh along at the sight of Ray encased within the curved rib bones, pretending to bang on them as if they were prison bars. Lauren's laugh was, of course, loudest of all. Only Lauren could still flirt whilst Dream Riding.

"This thing is awesome," Ray stated enthusiastically, appearing at their side once more. "Seriously, it's like, gigantic. Imagine what the Earth was like when these things were stomping around all over the place."

Kyra was astonished. It was possibly the most words she'd heard Ray speak in one sentence, and it was definitely the most animated she'd ever seen him.

"He's stunning, isn't he?" she agreed.

"Isn't he just?" murmured Lauren, who was gazing so intently at Ray that she didn't seem to have noticed the dinosaur at all.

Kyra and Crystal shared a smile but suppressed their laughter. Kyra wasn't sure Ray had even noticed Lauren's blatant flirting, though she couldn't imagine how.

"I know," Kyra added, attempting to get the conversation back on track, "I bet it was a beautiful sight. Lush and green and natural, each species doing just what it was meant to do to keep the intricate design of the world in balance. Wish I could see it for real some day."

Lauren gave her a look. "Seriously, Ky, what's going on with you? You sound more like Noah every day," she said, and winked to show she was joking.

"Why? Because I'm interested in something other than the opposite sex?" Kyra shot back with a smile, and was surprised by the image of Golden Boy that popped into her mind. Although to be honest, he'd never been far from her mind since she'd first seen him. Ignoring her friend's feigned expression of shock, she steered the conversation back on track. "Actually, we could learn a lot from dinosaurs, you know. We think we're so special, us humans. Dinosaurs happily ruled this planet for a hundred and fifty million years. Can you even imagine how long that is?" she asked nobody in particular.

"Are you serious? That's like, forever!" Crystal exclaimed as Kyra nodded eagerly, happy to finally be able to talk about something she knew a little about. "Hard to get your head 'round, isn't it? Humans in their very earliest form are only known to have been around for about a quarter of a million years – not even close to how long the dinosaurs existed. And look at all the damage we've done to the planet and our own race in that time. It's mind blowing!" It was a subject Kyra was passionate about. She couldn't understand how people spent so long worrying about how they looked, and how much money they had, yet failed to see the bigger picture.

"It sure is. That's crazy. Gee, why are we that way? People, I mean. When you look at it like that you realise we ain't gonna last much longer, not in the big scheme of things!" Ray assessed.

"Nope, you're right. Not unless something changes drastically."

The friends were all lost in their own silent reflections then, as they gazed around the hall and took in the other exhibits from their vantage point in the middle.

Lauren broke the silence. "Do you think that's what Dream Riders are for – to try and fix things – to make the world better?"

"You know what, Lauren? Crystal and I have been Dream Riding for a long time now, always trying to figure out what we're meant to do, you know, what it's all for. But I think you hit the nail on the head. From the things we've seen and the people we've met, I think that's exactly what Dream Riders are meant to do: to make things better. One small step at a time." Ray held eye contact with Lauren then, and Kyra realised she needed to intercept, worried that her best friend might actually just melt into a puddle of gooeyness.

"Okay, well, back to dinosaurs. Follow me. Let's see the rest of them," Kyra instructed and zoomed off down a corridor leading off from the main hall and then through a doorway on the left. It was like a different place than the museum she'd visited previously. Everything was so open and free to look at without hustle and bustle. She remembered how long they'd had to queue last time to see the dinosaur exhibition, her mother complaining every step of the way about her sore feet and her need for a coffee.

Kyra shook off the memory, and like a bird set free from a cage she soared upward to fly high above the suspended walkway that lead through the dinosaur hall. Feeling the others behind her with that sixth sense of just knowing, which she was fast growing accustomed to, she drifted slowly, imagining she herself was a pterodactyl. Taking in each and every one of the dinosaurs from her bird's eye view, skeletons and models, large and small, she studied them all carefully, knowing this experience was one she would never forget. The others found it as fascinating as she did and not even Lauren complained about the time Kyra took to soak up every last detail.

Finally reaching the end of the room, she swooped around to the right and looked at her favourite sight in the whole museum, the one she'd been waiting for. Gliding to a halt, she gazed at the scene before her and heard the others gasp in awe as they rounded the corner behind her. A life-sized T-Rex stood proudly before them, the rock and greenery surrounding him built carefully to replicate the environment in which he would have existed. Feeling slightly disappointed even though she'd expected it, Kyra noted that the electrical power was turned off at night time, making him not quite as impressive as he would have been with full sound and movement.

"He usually roars and swings his head around. Honestly, it's like you're really there, back in the Jurassic period! I mean, I guessed it wouldn't be turned on at night but I'd hoped so anyway."

"Hey, this is so cool just as it is. Check it out." Ray appeared suddenly atop the back of the enormous dinosaur pretending to ride it as if it were a horse. "Care for a ride m'lady?" he asked Lauren, patting the space behind him. Lauren hovered over, beaming, and perched on the broad back of the T-Rex behind him, although of course they weren't dense enough to actually make contact with the actual material of the exhibit and were really only floating above it.

They'd seen a whole new side to Ray since leaving her bedroom Kyra noted. It just goes to show, you can't always trust first impressions, she thought, and noticed Crystal smiling at her. She'd assumed Ray to be quiet and withdrawn when in fact, in the last twenty minutes, he'd proven himself to be something of a comic and not shy at all.

It was in that moment, as they were all in high spirits and messing around, that the mysterious shapes appeared, three of them, drifting like ashy smoke around the room. They were roughly the size of people, but completely formless, constantly shifting as they hovered sinisterly behind the T-Rex. A sudden change in atmosphere seemed to be directly linked to the dark shapes, as if they'd sucked all the light and joy from the room and were radiating the opposite, darkness and oppression. Lauren and Ray quickly appeared at Crystal's side just ahead of Kyra, and the Dream Riders watched the shadowy shapes in silent confusion.

After just a few short seconds, Kyra suddenly realised with alarm that she was fading, weakening, and losing her ability to focus, as if being slowly drained of all her energy. "Help, someone, help me... " she managed to call feebly with her mind. But her friends didn't hear her call, transfixed as they were by the shapes, which had now morphed into one large and murky blob.

Although her vision was dimming, the sudden appearance of her "boy at the window" right in front of her was like a full moon on a clear night - a beautiful vision. When their eyes fixed on each other, she experienced that breath-taking connection again, that inexplicable link, and was somehow aware of the healing golden light he was pouring into her through his strong and steady gaze, until she felt not only okay again, but more than okay. She felt refreshed, amazing! Looking him briefly up and down, she estimated he was probably around the same age as she, maybe slightly older.

"Thank you," she said, knowing he'd somehow fixed her. He smiled in response, setting her aglow. But before she could ask any of the questions she'd been forming all weekend, he was gone, just as quickly as he'd appeared; and she was left once again staring into the empty space he'd occupied.

"What the hell was that?" asked Ray, staring around him. Kyra snapped back to reality. "That was some freaky shit – it was like shadows floating around the room."

"Seriously freaky," Crystal agreed.

"They've gone now. They were probably nothing anyway. I mean, it's not as if this whole thing isn't extraordinary, right? We're bound to see and feel some weird stuff now and again. Don't you think?" Lauren asked and looked around for agreement.

Kyra thought she was probably right, and nodded. Now the room was back to normal, the shadow-shape-thingies didn't seem nearly as sinister in memory as they had been in reality.

More importantly to Kyra, however, was the fact that none of her friends seemed to have noticed her Golden Boy. She realised she'd been positioned behind the other three and their attention had been focussed on the shapes in the other direction. She also realised that she was glad. She wanted Golden Boy to remain her secret, for no reason at all other than to be able to cherish him without questions and speculation. She wanted him all to herself, and this time she had no doubt she'd see him again.

But what had happened to her? Something bad, she knew. That sensation of being depleted of all energy was scary and not something she wanted to experience again. She made a mental note to ask Noah about it, but her concern was dwarfed by the lingering glow of her Dream Riding saviour.

"Come on," she said with a smile. "Let's go. Who wants to check

out the mammals?"
    Everyone agreed.

Chapter 27

The time tunnel was short this time, which she assumed was due to the physical distance between locations being so small, but it was no less magical. Funny how things that seemed so hard to understand at first were starting to make sense, she thought. She supposed it was like everything, easier to understand in reality than in theory. When she emerged from the whirlpool of sparkles this time, she was hovering by an Indian elephant, exactly where she'd focussed her attention. It was less than a second before her three companions were by her side.

They explored the room thoroughly. It was yet another immense space, and they exclaimed over each animal and each little detail. The most impressive sight in this room, the one that was impossible to ignore, was the enormous blue whale replica, the largest mammal that had ever lived, so colossal in size it was almost beyond comprehension.

The foursome flew playfully through the massive model, imagining how it would feel to swim alongside such a beast in the depths of the ocean, and even to be swallowed whole and trapped in its guts. Only Lauren didn't find it amusing and eventually tired of the antics. "Okay, can we please do something interesting now? We've seen everything you wanted to, haven't we Kyra?"

Kyra was stunned. It wasn't that Lauren was snappy. She didn't mind that; she knew her friend didn't find this stuff interesting and had been as patient as she could. No, it was that Lauren had sounded so much like her mum. For a second she was drawn so far into a memory it almost took her breath away. She was transported back there, two years previously, not long before her parents had separated for good. They were in this exact room, in this exact spot, and Kyra's mother had said almost those exact words...

"Shall we go now dear, you've seen everything you wanted to, haven't you Kyra?" And then she'd looked at Kyra with that expression, as if daring Kyra to challenge her, or give her an answer she didn't want to hear. Kyra had just nodded, although disappointment had flared inside. She'd felt her father tense as he glared at her mother, felt the shift in the atmosphere between them. She'd been overcome with that feeling of walking on egg shells she always got when she sensed an argument brewing. It hadn't taken much to set them off in those days and she'd have done anything to avoid that bubbling pot of anger and resentment boiling over.

"Kyra?"

The voice snapped Kyra out of the memory and she planted a smile on her face. It was all history and she dto ruin this experience with negative memories.

"Come on, guys, I've seen enough. Let's go," she said.

"But, Kyra, where's Lauren?" They all gazed at the spot where Lauren had been just a few seconds earlier, but there was nothing there. She'd vanished.

Chapter 28

At first Lauren thought the whole room was fading away, but then she realised it wasn't fading. It was just kind of shifting. The process happened slowly, yet at the same time almost instantaneously. Everything dimmed slightly, losing its vibrancy, its saturation, until the whole room was almost monotone. Next, her friends seemed to dissolve right there in front of her. They just evaporated into thin air. Then all of a sudden, before she had time to wonder where they'd gone, everything burst into life again. It was as if somebody changed the settings of her vision, turning up both the brightness and the volume. And suddenly the room was awash with light and colour, movement and sounds. People appeared everywhere, hundreds of them, milling around, gasping and pointing, laughing and chatting, pushing past each other, and leaning over to get a better look at the display of African elephants, just metres from where she floated.

Lauren watched all of this with no shift in emotion at all. She was intrigued about what was occurring, but she wasn't scared. Completely baffled, but eager to understand, she felt instinctively that this was something she was supposed to experience. As she remained still, watching the unknowing people scurrying around, she puzzled over where they'd all materialised from, and to where her friends had disappeared. She figured if she wanted to she could follow them at will by just focusing on them as she'd practised with Crystal and Kyra. At least she *hoped* she could, but she wasn't ready yet. Something told her to wait a little while, to see what transpired.

Was it possible time had speeded up? That her friends had returned home and she had simply stayed in the museum, that it was now the following day and she'd been floating here all night? It seemed unlikely but as yet she was unable to think of another explanation. Just as she was beginning to feel slightly uneasy about this possibility, a voice caught her attention, a woman's voice, raised slightly higher than the others around her, a clipped voice. A voice she recognised said, "Shall we go now dear, you've seen everything you wanted to, haven't you, Kyra?"

Lauren peered, baffled, at the tall dark haired lady from whom the voice had emerged. She could only see her side on, but she was pretty sure. *Kyra's mother. What on Earth?* It was possible that if her theory about time speeding up was correct her friend's mother could have coincidentally visited the museum the following day? But why would Kyra be there too? Her confusion grew deeper. Unless, unless Kyra had come back to try to find her? But why wouldn't she have Dream Ridden? What the hell was going on? Lauren moved closer to the group just as she heard a male voice, speaking in quieter tones than Kyra's mother had done.

"You couldn't help yourself, could you? Not even just for one day. You just had to ruin it with your selfishness. Just like you ruin everything," he spat out the venomous words with force.

Lauren peered through the crowd and could see instantly, even from behind, that it was Kyra's father. With his too-long messy brown hair and that tweed jacket he wore everywhere, he was unmistakable. Now this really was impossible. Lauren knew her friend's parents only spoke to each other when necessary, and would absolutely *not* be visiting the museum, or anywhere, together.

Moving past the people who stood between her and Kyra's family, Lauren figured she could catch Kyra's eye, attract her attention somehow. She could see her friend standing away from her parents slightly, head down, obviously upset and also embarrassed as her mother's raised voice shot out again.

"Oh don't give me that. Just because you have no interests other than that bloody computer doesn't mean the rest of us aren't allowed lives."

People were turning to look now, wondering what the commotion was, but Lauren wasn't interested in Kyra's parents. She couldn't take her eyes off Kyra. She could tell, even from behind, that something wasn't right. Kyra was different. Smaller. Much smaller.

Suddenly Mr. Sutton strode away, taking Kyra's hand and pulling her with him. "Well come on then," he shot over his shoulder, "you've got it your way, let's go."

Lauren was shocked to see him so angry. She'd always known Kyra's father to be quiet and mild mannered. Now she really understood just how unhappy Kyra's parents had been before they separated. It illustrated perfectly everything her friend had ever told her about that bleak period in her life.

The Suttons marched down the corridor, and Lauren estimated that her friend was at least three inches shorter than she had been when she'd last seen her, not to mention the fact her hair had lost about four inches in length. Baffled, she decided at that point to stop thinking at all, and to simply observe. She could try and make sense of it all later.

Following them through a maze of corridors and then a café, Lauren was unable to hear the heated words that were obviously being exchanged. She simply kept her eyes fixed on Kyra. It was as they were entering the gift shop that she realised things were changing again. The colour was draining from around her once more. She heard Kyra's father ask, "Is it at least ok if we let her get something from the gift shop, or will that bore... " But the words sounded slow and laboured, as if they were travelling through some thick gloopy liquid, and then they were lost altogether.

The people around her were fading again, as was the sound. And then all volume was lost altogether. This time Lauren did feel a little spooked, and decided it was time to get out. Picturing

Kyra's bedroom in her head and remembering the mantra Crystal had taught her to use when she wanted to return to her body, she repeated, "I want to go to back to my body. I want to go back to my body." She repeated the mantra over and over again as she was suddenly and effortlessly swept though the time tunnel. Milliseconds later she opened her eyes and found four concerned faces intently peering down at her.

Chapter 29

"The weirdest thing just happened to me," Lauren said and promptly sat up. The others stared at her, astonished.

"Kyra, tell me, when you went to that museum last time with your mum and dad, were you wearing black jeans and these really bright red trainers and a grey and black striped jumper with Snoopy on the back?"

Kyra looked at her quizzically for a moment before instructing the group, "Okay, everyone move back a little, give her some space." As she helped Lauren to a sitting position, she asked, "Lauren, what happened? Did you have trouble getting back?" She was seriously worried now, scanning her friend for any obvious signs of physical injury, although she knew that was impossible.

"Ray, can you pass that glass of water, please?"

"No," Lauren waved a hand as if trying to disperse her friend's concern. "Stop fussing. I'm fine. Nothing happened. Nothing like that. Kyra, I'm serious, think back. Were you wearing the clothes I just described?"

Kyra gave her a dubious look and was quiet for a moment as she thought. Crystal and Noah perched on the edge of the bed, listening with curiosity as Ray, the glass of water still in his hand, just hovered at Lauren's side.

"I think so. Yes, yes, I was...I remember getting ready that morning. I was so excited, and that was my favourite outfit," Kyra replied as she confirmed Lauren's suspicions. But Lauren wanted to be absolutely sure.

"Ky, I hate to bring up bad memories but I have to check. Did your parents have a massive argument when you were there? Right in that room near the elephants? The grey African ones, not the Indian ones," she continued as she took hold of her Kyra's hand.

"They did actually," Kyra replied, not upset at all by the memory. It was history, done and dusted, and everyone was happy now. "Mum wanted to leave. She was bored. It started a row. I was thinking about that while we were there, just before you disappeared. How did you....wait....did you read my mind? Can you do that too – like Crystal?" Kyra's eyes were wide, excited.

"No, no I don't think so. It's something else... " Lauren went on to explain how she seemed to have been sucked right into Kyra's memory and had found herself watching the scene unravelling before her eyes. She described every second, every word, in as much detail as she could remember, right up until the point she had willed herself back into her body. Four faces gaped in wonder, their owners struggling to understand what had transpired.

"Damn, that's unbelievable. It's exactly what happened, just as you described it. I didn't even remember half of it. Wow! How the hell did you do that?" Kyra asked. Only Noah's expression was one of delight, and he moved toward Lauren, addressing her directly as he spoke.

"Lauren, this is fantastic. You're a Traveller."

She just looked at him blankly, hoping an explanation would follow, as seemed to be Noah's style. Make a statement and then explain it.

"Okay, let's talk tools," he said and looked around at their bewildered faces.

"Noah, it's hardly the time to be discussing DIY – what..." Kyra began, confused. But she stopped when Noah began laughing so hard he looked like he might pee himself. The others looked on, as baffled as Kyra, but intrigued too.

"I didn't mean those kinds of tools," he said when he had finally got his laughter under control. "I meant tools as in the special gifts some Riders have, like Lauren's. Sorry, I'm getting ahead of myself. I should explain." He sat down on the desk chair and Ray finally handed the glass of water to an open mouthed Lauren and then slid to the spot of floor next to her. All eyes were on Noah.

"There are a variety of tools that I know of, but not all Dream Riders have one. Lauren, I believe you're a Traveller. That's the common name. The full name is a *Memory Traveller*."

"Wait, that's kind of like a time traveller, right?" Lauren looked excited now. "But don't you need some kind of time machine for that? Like the car in *Back to the Future* or the telephone box in *Doctor Who*. Are you serious – I travelled in time? 'Cause I kind of thought I had, but then I thought you'd all laugh at me for being stupid. Please don't all laugh at me. Put me out of my misery, Noah. Did I travel in time?"

Noah finally caught a long enough break to actually get a few words in edgeways. "Yes, Lauren, I think you did," he affirmed. And then he added, "In a way."

Lauren sucked in an excited breath, covering her mouth with both her hands as she waited for the explanation.

"It's kind of a deceptive name," Noah continued, "because you didn't really travel anywhere at all. You merely tuned in to a different time frequency. How can I explain this?" He tapped his fingers on the desk and looked to the ceiling as if for inspiration while the rest of the group waited eagerly.

"Okay, just think of it like this: Kyra was thinking of a situation that happened in her past. Her memory was formed largely from the energy of that time, that event. You tuned into that energy and, in your capacity as a Traveller, your consciousness was transported to the event and all the associated energies that constructed it – the physical energies of the place, the objects, the people, the sound energies, and so on. So you could view that event as if you were actually there. Following me?"

Lauren let out a stream of breath. "I think I kind of might be. But,

I mean...wow! So this isn't just a one off? I could do it again?"

"Well yes, theoretically you could attach yourself to the energy of any memory and travel there. Although, like all tools, it may take some practice to control," Noah explained patiently.

Lauren considered this. "I think I might give it a while before I try again. It was totally cool, but I'm kind of on new experience overload at the moment. I think I'll just keep practicing the Dream Riding for now and think about travelling to people's memories later!" she smiled.

"That's fine. You shouldn't force any of this. There's no rush. Everything will happen in perfect timing just when it's supposed to. Just do what feels right, *when* it feels right," Noah answered as he returned her smile. "Oh, and just so you know, it doesn't have to be a memory of a person. That's the exciting bit. A place can hold memory energy too, which you can also tune into."

"Sweet," muttered Ray.

Kyra couldn't help noticing he'd reverted back to Mr Silent since they'd returned.

"So, did she or did she not travel in time?" asked Kyra, the only one of the group who dared speak so bluntly to Noah.

"Yes and no. Yes, in that she was conscious of a 'time' and 'date' other than that of her current reality. No, in that time doesn't really exist as a place that you can 'go,'" Noah said.

"Okay, so let's not get into all that again. It gave me a bad enough headache the first time," Crystal joked.

"Yeah this stuff is deep," Ray agreed. "So, Lauren's tool is Travelling. How about the rest of us?"

"Well, like I said, not all Riders have tools. But I think in this group you're pretty lucky. Firstly, Kyra, there's your tool," Noah said, and all attention shifted to Kyra, who squirmed under the scrutiny.

"Mine? What do you mean? What's mine?" she asked, genuinely stunned.

"You know, connecting. With the spirit world. With spirits. You're a *Connector*, Kyra. That's your tool."

Of course, Kyra thought. It was all making sense. Talking to her dead grandmother and being able to fly were linked. She was fast learning there was no such thing as a coincidence.

"But I only communicate with my Nana, not *spirits* as in plural!"

"That doesn't matter. You still connect to the spirit world. I bet if the situation required it you could communicate with other spirits too. But tools are for a reason, and they will come into play only when required. So for now you've been communicating with your Nana Anna while you Dream Ride. And I bet she's been preparing you for whatever's to come."

Kyra considered this, and had to agree. She'd always had a sense that her Nana was getting her ready for something. She'd just never understood what. Now all was becoming clear, but something Noah had said bothered her. "You said I communicate with her during Dream Rides...that's true. But I can also see her and talk to her when I'm not Riding."

Noah's eyes grew wide. "Really? For how long?" He leaned forward and put a hand on Kyra's arm, looking serious suddenly. She was slightly alarmed. Had she said something wrong?

"Well, like, since I was five."

"Kyra, that's fantastic. You're a *Switcher*. I've read so much about them. Apparently it's quite rare... "

"You what? A *Switcher*? This gets weirder by the minute! Go on then, what's a *Switcher*?" she asked, wondering how much odder her life could get.

It was as if she had been dropped into some fascinating secret world, much like Alice in *Alice in Wonderland* when she went down the rabbit's hole, Kyra imagined. There was so much to take in, so much to learn. She was so chuffed that Noah was on the team now and knew all this stuff. It was just so perfect.

"A Switcher is a person who can switch their energy frequency to the level required to use their tool without having to actually leave the physical body. Still with me?" he raised his eyebrows questioningly.

Kyra nodded slowly. She thought she understood so far. "So usually people only reach such a high energy frequency when they're in their energy body?"

"Exactly...for most Dream Riders it's impossible to control physical functions *and* use their tools, which is why they leave the physical body – it's too low, too dense. Tools require higher, lighter energy – like Dream Riding energy." He paused for a second, to make sure everyone was following him and absorbing his words.

"Switchers are able to switch between those energy frequencies at such a rapid speed it's imperceptible. Meaning they can use their tool and still remain in the physical, doing normal things like moving and talking."

"Wow!" Lauren exclaimed. "That's amazing. So Kyra, you're, like, even more special than normal, boring Dream Riders! Beats the hell out of my time travelling – sorry, memory travelling!" she joked and Kyra blushed, embarrassed.

"You really do know a lot of stuff, Noah. I knew you were brainy but I had no idea you were *this* clever," Kyra pointed out, trying to divert the attention away from herself.

"Well, we geeks sure do like to read," he joked, making light of the compliment. "You know, there are quite a variety of tools. They're referred to as tools because that's what they are – tools you can use to help you with whatever it is that needs to be done."

"That's so cool, so what... " Lauren began, but Noah cut her off with a smile.

"...other tools are there? Didn't have to be a *Reader* to know you were going to ask that! Which answers your question nicely. There are Readers – they can read thoughts – I gather you're a Reader, Crystal?" Another piece of knowledge he'd picked up whilst eavesdropping – something he wasn't proud of but didn't regret for a second.

"Well yes, I guess I am! I had no idea there was a name for it. How cool!" Crystal sat up straighter. Like all of them, she was obviously fascinated to learn these facts and was listening with intrigue to Noah's every word.

"And I've heard it works both ways, right? So you can put thoughts and images into people's heads as well as reading their thoughts?" Noah asked.

"Guilty!" Crystal grinned. "Yes, I can pretty much transmit thought waves to anyone while I'm Dream Riding. I mean, I can't like control their minds or anything, but I can show words and images to people. Like this." She was quiet for a minute, and dream riding out of her body, she transmitted an image to Noah, returning to her body with a smile when she saw his eyes widen.

"A fairy cake with pink icing?" he asked and she laughed.

"Yep, that's what I showed you."

"Oh, cool, that's gotta be fun!" Lauren stated. "What else is there Noah? Tell us more!"

"There are other tools too, but I'll bore you if I go into them all. I'm going to shut up now and let you get on with the meeting," Noah said, flushing with embarrassment at having completely dominated the whole conversation. Kyra knew how much he hated to be the centre of attention.

"No, you can't just tease us like that and not tell us the other tools," Lauren protested.

"Lauren, give the poor guy a break. We have plenty of time to learn all there is to learn," Kyra said. "I don't know about anybody else, but I for one am starving. Shall we raid the kitchen?"

The suggestion was a popular one and all five trooped down the stairs and into the kitchen where Kyra's dad was making himself a cup of tea. Kyra explained away her guests by muttering something about a group assignment at school, and Noah added that he was helping out as it was a topic he'd covered at his school the previous term.

Mr. Sutton was either satisfied with the explanation or too busy thinking about his website to care, as he shuffled out with a distracted nod of the head, calling out behind him, "Noah, when you've got a minute could you nip in to take a look at a module I'm working on?"

Kyra smiled and shook her head, amused. Ten minutes later they were settled back on the floor of Kyra's bedroom, ready for the next adventure. The spotlight was on Lauren.

"Where to, Miss Lockett?"

"Where else? We're going backstage…at The Wanted's Concert!!"

Chapter 30

The brief but heavy rain shower had passed, and although a herd of thinning clouds still strolled across the sky, intermittent patches of clear blue were also now visible. This is good, Marco thought, peering through the kitchen window. It meant he wouldn't have to get drenched when he met up with the lads later.

Walking to the cooker, one hand encased in a striking floral oven glove, he retrieved a tray of overdone fish fingers and chips, and used his free hand to sweep them onto the two plates he'd laid out in preparation, wincing painfully as the heat bit his fingertips. After adding the baked beans he'd already warmed up, he called in the general direction of the hallway, "Dad, dinner's ready."

Depositing the baking tray and saucepan in the sink, he filled them with hot water to soak and then carried the two plates to the table in the dining area, placing them down and surveying his handiwork. Never a day passed without him wondering why he went to all this trouble. The place mats, the cutlery, the water jug, and glasses, all neatly arranged on the small round table, just as they were almost every evening. Yet the result was always the same.

"Dad, are you coming?" he shouted a few minutes later, his voice now laced with resentment. He was already sitting down and digging into his crunchy feast. The keen servitude under which he'd made his dad's meal was diminishing and being fast replaced by anger. His old man was an arse, simple as that. He'd never come to the table for his meal while Marco was there, and Marco knew it. But he'd sure as hell eat the bloody food while Marco was out. There was no doubt in the boy's mind about that. As he continued to chew his food mechanically, now burning with anger, Marco had a quiet bet with himself that his dad's currently untouched plate would be spotless by the time he returned home tonight. It would be sitting right there in exactly the same position on the table, but it would be completely empty.

The sound of the toilet flushing interrupted his train of thought, and a naive flash of hope flared inside him, taking him by surprise. Was his dad coming to the dining room after all? Were they actually going to sit down together? Maybe even talk to each other? Thinking back, he realised he couldn't remember the last time they'd had anything even remotely resembling a conversation. And as his father's footsteps plodded down the stairs, he felt a nervous flurry in his stomach at the prospect of the silence ending. Reaching the bottom, Marco's father glanced right. From his position at the foot of the stairs he had a clear view of Marco sitting at the table, his eyebrows raised and his expectant expression of hope so eager it was almost pathetic. Turning away as if he hadn't even seen his son, Luca DiCarmello took slow laboured strides into the lounge.

He's an arse, simple as that, Marco repeated to himself silently. The anger had returned, and he was now stabbing each mouthful of chips onto his fork with menacing force as though the harmless potato chunks were the source of all his woes. A knock at the door snapped Marco out of his dark mood, the promise of tonight's entertainment triggering a half smile. Leaving his unfinished plate at the table, he rushed to the kitchen door and pulled it open.

"Alright, Spam," he greeted the teenage boy. Spam was a little taller than Marco with a larger build and a short fuzz of white-blonde hair. Marco knew the older boy hated the nickname, but he didn't give a toss. He'd sussed him out a long time ago. Spam used to have a reputation for being hard and reckless, and Marco had used the tough guy to enhance his own renown. But the key to getting in with the older lad had been realising that Spam was in fact a pussy. He might scare a lot of other kids, but it hadn't taken Marco long to realise he was all talk and no balls.

"You ready or what?" Spam mumbled. "We gotta meet Jez in a couple of minutes."

"Yeah, you got the eggs, Spam?" Marco inquired. He never bought the ammunition for this kind of thing himself. He wasn't stupid enough to get caught with anything incriminating on him. Instead he always sent one of his mates into the shop for eggs, spray cans, fireworks, whatever. There was always someone either eager to score brownie points with Marco, or just too pussy to say no. This time they'd be heading to the foot bridge over the motorway, and Marco was genuinely excited.

"Course I've got em. I ain't thick you know." Spam frowned and straightened himself up, but took a step backward at the same time.

"Yes, you bloody are!" exclaimed Marco and shoved the other lad roughly on the shoulder. Spam looked down silently and Marco shook his head in disgust, thinking he's so gay. Grabbing his hoodie from where he'd dumped it on the counter earlier, he shouted, "Later, Dad."

In the lounge his father stared silently at the television, completely unmoved as the back door slammed shut.

Chapter 31

"He is SUCH a babe! Oh my God, I'm so hyped!" Lauren exclaimed and collapsed back on Kyra's bed with a sigh.

"Lauren Lockett, hyped? Never!" Kyra smiled sarcastically.

"He is pretty good looking though, isn't he?" Crystal added.

"It was unreal. It was the most amazing moment of my life, seriously. If I died right now I would die one happy bunny. I can't believe I was there. My heart nearly stopped when I saw them, and we were so *close*." Lauren jumped to her feet again.

"I guess it was pretty awesome," Ray agreed. "I mean, totally not my kind of thing, but they did put on a good show."

Kyra couldn't believe it. Was she the only person who'd noticed? Everything had gone wrong at the concert. Tom had tripped just as he was heading on stage. The microphones had been screeching with feedback half the time, and one of the stage hands had almost dropped a lighting rig onto the live stage. Kyra had spent most of her time at the concert clenching her teeth and waiting for disaster to strike. The Wanted? More like The Wanting!

"Oh, come on guys, it wasn't that good! Was I at a completely different concert than the rest of you?"

They all turned and looked at her, wearing the kind of expressions she would have expected to see if she'd just announced she was taking up sumo wrestling or opening a donkey retreat.

"Come on, Kyra. It was a fantastic show, you have to admit it!" Crystal said.

"Yeah, and isn't Max just the biggest hottie you have ever seen? Did you see how sweaty he was when he ran backstage to change his shirt that time? Soooo sexy." Lauren slumped back down on the bed, a huge grin lighting up her face.

"Ewww, Lauren, that's sick." Kyra scrunched up her nose in disgust.

"You're just jealous because Jay didn't stare into *your* eyes and serenade you," her friend replied.

"Lauren, you were hovering in front of him, and he couldn't see you. You were invisible. I hate to burst your bubble, but he *so* wasn't singing to you," Kyra said with an exasperated roll of her eyes. "Next time, we can go to the National Gallery, and see some *real* talent."

"So anyway, whose turn is it next?" asked Noah, who had been silently watching the exchange with amusement. He wasn't sorry to have missed this one; he definitely sided with Kyra in the entertainment preference stakes.

"Nope, nobody is next, we're all done. Ray and I have pretty much been there, done that, got the T-shirt. So that's everybody," Crystal smiled.

"Well actually, not everybody," Noah replied. "I know I can't Dream Ride yet; but as I'm now an official member of the group, I wondered if I could have a turn. And if you'd mind taking my turn for me?" His question was greeted by four expressions of mild surprise. But before anyone could answer, he added, "You see, I was sitting here wondering what I would do, where I would go, if I could. And I knew the answer immediately." The truth was, his contemplation had been spurred by a text message – from Marco.

He'd been having the absolute best evening of his entire life, finally having found the first step on his path to destiny, and he couldn't have been happier. But one little text from Marco had ruined it completely, bringing him back down with a bump, causing fear to seep back into his veins. That was when he'd decided exactly what he would do if he could be invisible.

Chapter 32

By the time they arrived at the foot bridge over the A27, the heavens had opened up, and Marco and his mates were now thoroughly sodden. Seriously, that kind of wet-as-you-can-get, soaked-to-the-bone type sodden. So much for the hopeful blue patches of sky. Instead, dense black cloud coverage had brought an early night to the south coast. Marco thought he'd be annoyed about the rain; but he soon realised the heavy downpour and dark sky served to disguise their presence, with the motorists down below concentrating harder on their driving and pedestrians unlikely to be passing by in this weather. The other boys might not have thought too much about cover, but Marco liked to be a step ahead. He liked to be in control.

Of the three figures standing on the bridge above the rushing cars, Marco was the first to speak up. "Alright, lads, who's up first?"

His friends both remained standing silently, hands in pockets. One of the boys was almost comically larger than the other, both looked sheepish. Marco had guessed he'd have to go first, but he couldn't resist the opportunity to embarrass the boys and to remind them of his status as the most daring, of his commanding position. His eyes flitted from one to the other, his expression one of disdain. "Well that's a surprise, not a pair of balls between you. Give me the bloody bag, Jez."

The scrawny boy who handed over the Tesco bag with a shaking hand appeared to be another product of the Wannabe Factory: tracksuit bottoms tucked into socks, football T-shirt hanging from his skinny shoulders. The kid's scruffy orange hair and freckles made him look like a naughty-boy caricature.

Marco pulled the carton from the bag and took out an egg. "This is how it's done, boys," he said smugly. Walking boldly to the shoulder-high barrier he gazed below at the onrushing traffic. Beams of light pierced the darkness as the lashing rain was illuminated in the headlights of each passing car, and spray whooshed up from beneath the tires. He planted one hand on the edge of the barrier, the egg held carefully in the other. Pulling his arm back behind his head he prepared to throw. Before making his move he looked over his shoulder and reminded his friends of the plan. "Remember if you hear any screeching tires, make a break for it and we'll meet back in the woods." The other boys nodded in confirmation, masks of bravado failing to hide the fear in their faces.

Marco launched the egg as hard as he could. It spun quickly through the air. Although the rain was lashing down, he could still see the egg's descent. And Marco thought to himself, Bullseye, as it found its target, landing harmlessly on the grass verge just beyond the hard shoulder. His friends were hanging back, still not daring to look over, as Marco turned to face them and shouted, "Got him," raising a fist triumphantly in the air. Jez and Spam looked at each other nervously as Marco continued bragging, "I don't know how that bastard's still driving. Must be his windscreen wipers or something, 'cause I definitely got him right in the middle! I tell ya lads, I'm far too good at this." He paused and stepped toward the other boys. "Right lads, who's up next? No chickening out now."

Spam pushed Jez forward, saying, "Go on, you're next" with a shaking voice.

Not wanting to appear to be a pussy in front of Marco, Jez took an egg and walked to the edge. Crouching down with his back to the barrier, he psyched himself up, terrified of actually throwing the egg, horrified at the thought of a possibly tragic outcome.

"Come on, you little tosser. Stop being such a baby," jibed Marco. Jez gritted his teeth and threw the egg in a backward arc, high over his head. Unable to actually look at the consequence of his action, he remained in his crouched position until Marco, standing over him but not yet looking over the edge, ordered him otherwise.

"Come on, get up and have a look at your handiwork. Thrower gets first look."

Tentatively, not wanting to lose any more face, and buoyed by the fact he hadn't heard any screeching tires or angry voices, Jez stood and peered over the grey barrier. What he saw drained the little colour from his face that was actually visible on this dim evening, and he looked both terrified and perplexed all at once. "What the... " A couple of metres away from the barrier, suspended above the onrushing cars, the egg hung unbelievably suspended in the air above the traffic. "Lads, you wanna come see this... "

Marco rushed toward the edge, frowning. There had obviously been no crash. What the hell was the little prick playing at? Before he could see properly over the barrier, or focus on what lay beyond the pouring rain, the wild egg suddenly started rushing back toward them with frightening speed.

"Oh...my... " were the only words Jez managed to squeak.

Marco and Spam still hadn't seen what he was looking at. Leaning over the edge and squinting into the darkness, Marco searched eagerly for what the small boy was harping on about. He was rewarded by the egg smacking him full force right between the eyes.

Cracking on contact, the shell fell to the ground and the gloopy raw contents slithered down his nose, mixing with a river of rain water. Stunned, Marco looked at his friends, who both looked as startled as each other.

"Who did that?" shouted an infuriated Marco, his eyes flashing with rage.

"It did it itself, Marco," Jez insisted in a whiny voice.

"What the hell do you take me for?" Marco angrily wiped the slimy egg from his face, growing more livid by the second. Where the hell had that egg come from? He knew it couldn't have been his friends; they'd been way behind him. He grabbed Jez by the scruff of the neck and the boy whimpered as Spam took a step backward. "I swear if you're lying to me... "

Marco glanced up at Spam to give him the same warning, and he noticed the boy was staring open mouthed at a spot somewhere above Marco's head.

"Oh...My...God... " Spam murmured.

Marco shouted, "What?" Tilting his head back, mouth gaping, he saw another egg, this time poised perfectly in mid air directly above his head. Squinting against the still heavy torrent of rain, he barely had time to let out a tiny gasp of surprise before the egg cracked, seeming to implode into itself, dribbling more raw egg into his eyes and over his face. "What the...what the...what the... " He couldn't form the rest of the sentence, and he turned to his friends, his eyes wide with fear and astonishment as the broken shell landed harmlessly on his sopping hair.

As Marco shook his head in disbelief, Spam shouted, "Leave him alone!" to Marco in a threatening tone he'd never dared use on the renowned nutter before. The other boys turned to stare at him, open mouthed.

"What the hell are you talking about?" Marco demanded furiously.

"Just leave him alone, you have to leave him alone and never hassle him again," Spam said slowly, pronouncing each word very definitively.

"What? Who are you talking about? Who did this?" Marco asked, sounding less sure of himself now.

"Noah," Spam replied.

"You what, what are you talking about?" There was definitely a distinct note of fear in Marco's voice now.

"I don't know. I don't know what I'm saying. I'm just saying what I see. For some reason I just know you should never hassle him again," Jez said, shaking his head in confusion.

"Or what?" Marco asked, defiant.

"Or that... " Spam said, pointing a shaking finger at the plastic bag, lying in a deep puddle of dirty rainwater, from which three eggs were now rising up slowly.

Marco had never felt such terror in all his life. He let a high pitched wail, more feline than human, and he didn't even recognise the sound as having from his own mouth. He didn't notice that Jez had quietly fainted beside him. He didn't understand why or how this was happening, but he knew he had to get out of there before those crazy bewitched eggs got him. Without a further glance at his friends, Marco sprinted toward the stairs at the end of the footbridge, sure that the mad eggs were flying after him.

Chapter 33

"Oh My God, Ray, that was so cool! How on Earth did you do it?" Lauren jumped to her feet, staring at Ray in awe. They were all staring at Ray in awe, with one exception.

"Do what?" asked a baffled Noah from his position on the desk chair. The others, besides Lauren who was now pacing up and down the room, were sitting on the floor, exactly where they'd been when they returned from the dream ride.

"Oh, Noah, the eggs – you should have seen it. Ray, that was amazing. What happened? Did you see the look on his face? It was hilarious!" Kyra said. She had to admit she'd got a lot of satisfaction seeing the tables turned on Marco.

"What was hilarious?" asked Noah.

"Marco was completely freaking out. Seriously, Noah, it was amazing. Ray, how did you do that? In all these years I have never seen you do something like that before!" Crystal chipped in. "Have you been keeping something from me?"

"No, I swear, Crys, I had no idea, when I saw that egg, I just... " Ray began.

"Just what? What the hell happened?" Noah shouted, standing up. The other four looked up at him, stunned. "Can somebody please let me in on this fascinating little recount, because I wasn't there, remember?" Then, looking suddenly embarrassed, he sat back down. "Sorry, it's just; I just want to know."

"It's okay. Noah, sorry. God, we're so insensitive. It was your dream ride after all. Sorry," Kyra said, and the others nodded in agreement. "Okay, you wanted Marco to leave you alone. Well I'm pretty certain he will after this." She smiled at him, and could see in his eyes how eager he was to hear every detail. She recounted how they'd found Marco easily by just thinking of him, there on the footbridge high above Courtwood Road. She described how they'd reached him just in time to see him throwing the first egg over the side and how it had landed harmlessly at the roadside despite his false claim of hitting the car.

"God, he is actually really dangerous. I can't believe he was egging cars. Stupid idiot. I knew he was a bully, but that's just way beyond what I thought he was capable of. He could have killed someone!"

Noah was horrified, as the rest of them had been, to discover what Marco got up to out of school hours.

"He was up to his usual tricks though, pushing around two kids from school. I recognised them but don't know their names. They all looked so pathetic up there, like drowned rats with their wet hair plastered to their foreheads," Kyra sniggered at the memory, as Noah listened intently, hungrily soaking up every word.

"So then he ordered the smallest boy to do it, and you could see the poor kid was flippin' terrified. He threw the egg backward. He couldn't even look. And I thought he was actually going to cry."

"And this is the amazing bit. This is where Ray saved the people in the car. It was like something out of a film. A proper hero. Honestly, Noah, it was so cool," Lauren interrupted, and smiled brilliantly at Ray as she talked. Ray buried his head in his hand, embarrassed, as the other two girls laughed. Lauren, as usual, was completely oblivious to both Ray's discomfort and the sheer comedy of her brazen admiration.

"Okay, I believe you, Lauren. Ray was amazing. Maybe Ray should tell the next bit?" Noah prompted Ray with raised eyebrows.

"Oh, yeah, sure." Ray began. "Well when I saw the second egg go over I knew I had to do something. We could all see where it was headed – straight into the traffic. There was a station wagon below and the egg was flying toward the windscreen. I just...I... it's so hard to explain. I kind of imagined myself catching the egg and next thing I knew there I was, hovering above the road as the station wagon zoomed past, with the egg cupped in my hand."

"In your hand?" Noah repeated.

"Yeah, dude, in my hand. I know. I don't get it either – the egg is solid right? But somehow it happened. Then I saw the kid looking over the barrier, so I thought this could like be the perfect opportunity to scare them – just to stop them from being so dumb. So I hovered up with the egg in my hand."

"It was hilarious, Noah. This boy looked completely freaked out. He could barely even talk. And then Marco looked over and Ray just threw the egg at him. Like, right at his face," Lauren interrupted again.

Kyra thought she'd better summarise or they would be here all day.

"Yeah, then he got really mad and thought somehow one of the other boys had done it. So Ray picked up another egg and broke it above his head to distract him. Then Crystal stepped in, and started putting thoughts in this other boy's head and making him talk – like saying, 'Leave Noah alone.' Did you know Readers could do that, Noah?"

Noah was just looking stunned. This was hilarious, better than anything he could have hoped for. "Well, uh, yeah. I know as well as reading thought waves, they can transmit them into another person's mind. But it's not as simple as putting thoughts in their head, or making them talk. I'm guessing you're able to just show them images. Right, Crystal?"

"Exactly," Crystal agreed. "I was struggling to explain it to the others before. I just show images to a person – in this case I showed the boy an image of the words – and he chose to say them out loud. It's not like I can control people's minds or anything."

Noah had turned to the computer and launched a web browser,

where he was typing in an address. He spoke without looking back, partly because he was welling up, "Guys, I don't know what to say. I'm so grateful for what you've done I can never thank you enough. Honestly, you don't know what a difference this will make in my life."

Kyra walked over to stand behind him and squeezed his shoulder gently. She didn't need to say any words. Her own emotions were a reflection of Noah's. And although the others hadn't known Noah as long as she, they were all proud to have been able to help him and put their gifts to good use.

"So, what're you doing?" Kyra asked after Noah had typed in a series of passwords and followed links between several web pages.

"I thought it might be useful for us to discover what Ray's tool is," he replied.

"Oh, you mean you don't know?"

"Believe it or not Ky, I don't know everything," Noah laughed. "I had heard some Dream Riders have the ability to affect physical matter, but I don't think it's well documented, meaning it must be rare." Noah was now browsing through a site, looking for something. "Nope, it's definitely not on here under the tools section, and this is currently the main resource. Although who knows for how long. These sites are always closing down and moving."

"Really? Why's that?" asked Crystal. The four Dream Riders had created a semi circle behind Noah, all interested in learning more about Ray's tool.

"I have no idea. I've tried asking but nobody talks about it. These sites are hard enough to find anyway, and even harder to get into. When they disappear it's a royal pain in the arse to find them again," Noah replied. "Okay, here we go. I posted the question, and look, somebody has answered already.

"'The ability to affect physical matter is apparently known as 'Moving,'" he read. "So, Ray, you are a Mover."

"Ha, I like it, kind of cool!" Ray said, popping his shirt collar with a smile.

"Yeah, not very original though, huh? So, okay look here, he's telling us more – according to this person, EnergyKing0860, "Moving" works by the Mover's energy becoming dense enough to clash with the physical matter, but not so dense that it can see seen by those in physical bodies," Noah explained, as he read from the screen and elaborated to clarify the explanation. "So, say you want to touch something with your hand, an egg for example, the energy that makes up your hand will become denser."

"Well that is pretty sweet. So how come I couldn't do it before?"

"You probably could have done it, but you didn't need to. Some Riders seem to only discover their tools when the situation calls for it. There are no rules though. The more I find out, the more I realise everyone is completely different."

"Hey, we all have tools now," Lauren observed. "Well, all of us who can dream ride at least," she added, looking at Noah sheepishly.

"It's okay," he smiled. "Honestly, I'm fine with it. I'll keep practising and if it's meant to happen it will. And yes, I'd say you guys are a pretty proficient dream riding group. You must be destined for something big!" he joked.

"Hey, don't exclude yourself from that Noah. We'd be nowhere without your input," Crystal added, and everyone agreed.

"Oh My God, look at the time. I have to get home or my mother will go mental," Lauren exclaimed, suddenly noticing the clock. She jumped up and began gathering her things.

"Yeah, but we've done pretty well. Who would have thought it possible to visit the Natural History Museum, a Jonas Brothers concert, and end the reign of a tyrant like Marco all in the space of four hours?" Kyra asked.

"I have a feeling tonight was just a taster," Crystal added.

They all had the same feeling. A sense of anticipation charged the air as the group of dream riders parted company that evening. Just as Noah was about to leave, a thought struck Kyra.

"Noah, wait, there's something else." She explained to him about the strange shadows they'd seen in the museum and the way she'd felt so depleted of her energy while they were there. "Have you heard of them before?" she asked. "Any idea what they might be?"

"None whatsoever. But I left that website open on your computer. Let's have a look."

Back in her room, using the chat box, Noah relayed Kyra's explanation of the shadows to EnergyKing0860 who was still online and asked if he knew anything about them.

Are you crazy? Don't talk about Phantoms online, not if you value your life.

Kyra felt her heart race and she looked at Noah in shock.

"What the... " he muttered and started to type again. When he clicked Shout to post his question, the web page displayed an eerie message telling them: "This page cannot be found." It didn't matter how many times he clicked refresh or tried to get back to the forum. The website had simply disappeared.

Chapter 34

Are you lonesome tonight...do you miss me tonight...
The crooning voice seemed at first to be part of her dream, a very pleasant dream in which she was swirling high above an icy landscape dancing with Golden Boy amongst the breathtaking spectacle of the Northern Lights. However, although she had never heard Golden Boy's voice, she thought these dulcet tones couldn't possibly belong to him, for his voice would surely be as light as the tinkle of a bell. As the singing tugged Kyra from her sleep, it dawned on her that she was actually listening to an Elvis number, which could mean only one thing. She opened one eye to find Nana Anna perched on the edge of her bed.

Something had changed.

"You look different," she said groggily, sitting up and leaning against the headboard. "Why are you here so early anyway?" She rubbed her eyes in an attempt to wake herself more fully.

"Well, that's a lovely greeting isn't it? Good Morning to you too, my cherub," Nana Anna replied with a twinkle in her eye, and continued to stroke Sooty.

"Sorry," Kyra smiled. "Good morning, Nana Anna," she said. And then she suddenly realised what was different. "You're wearing a different dress. Oh My God – you never wear different clothes. I thought, you know, you had to wear that flowery dress you're always in."

"I certainly do not." Offence laced her grandmother's voice. "I can wear whatever I like! And the best thing is, I don't need money to buy new clothes. I just think them up!" she beamed. "I just happen to like that purple dress. But I thought, given the occasion, it was time for some new attire to celebrate."

"The occasion – which occasion?"

"The formation of your group, of course. Kyra, I'm so very proud of what you've achieved recently. You've come so far!" she beamed wider still.

"Thank you, Nana. Yeah, it's been a pretty crazy few days."

"It certainly has, and there is more yet to come. I saw the deeds you were doing yesterday with your new friends. Good deeds. With good intentions."

"I didn't see you. Where were you?" Kyra asked, surprised.

"You don't always see me, darling," she smiled mysteriously. "Anyway, I just popped by to say hello. And to say that your business is unfinished."

"Huh? Which business?" Kyra asked. Maybe it was just because she hadn't woken up properly, but she could swear Nana Anna was acting very strangely indeed today.

"Your business with the poor DiCarmello boy. You need to pay him a visit. You don't really need me to help you now; you've found your own way. But it's hard, you know, hard to stop meddling when you love somebody."

Kyra was frowning in confusion. What the hell was her grandmother going on about? Was it possible to go senile after you were already dead?

"Okay, I have to run I'm afraid. I have an appointment. Toodle pip." And with that she was gone, leaving Kyra open mouthed and stunned. She ran the conversation over in her head a few times trying to memorise it for later analysis. Then she thought of her dream riding diary. Perfect. She jotted down everything she could remember and hoped it might actually be of some use.

Later, in the school cafeteria, the others were just as baffled as she was.

"The poor DiCarmello boy? Poor, after what he did to Noah? What's that all about?" Lauren asked. Nobody had an answer. But they all agreed they didn't want to discuss it any further without Noah present.

"Well, how about you all come over to our house tonight?" Crystal asked. "Kyra, surely your dad will start getting pissed soon if we all keep barging in every night. Lauren, will you be able to get away again?" She'd already clocked that Lauren had the strictest parents amongst the group.

"Yep, I told the parents last night we were all working on an assignment for drama, and they, like, totally believed me. That'll keep me going for a while. Then I'll think of something else."

"And I have no problem with that – dad and Liam can fend for themselves! I'll text Noah too. Will your parents be ok with it?" Kyra asked, realising they still knew little about Crystal and Ray's family aside from the fact the pair seemed to have a lot of freedom.

"Oh, totally. No worries there," Crystal smiled, sipping apple juice through a straw.

As Crystal explained the directions to their house, Kyra thought how nice it felt to be a part of a group for the first time ever, a proper group that could claim a whole table in the canteen. She smiled to herself as the bell for the end of lunch break rang and strode proudly from the cafeteria with the rest of the group walking alongside her. She was aware in her peripheral vision of the envious looks being cast their way and held her head high.

Chapter 35

The first thing the Visitor was aware of as he returned to his body was the thudding of his heart. Fear had him in its icy grasp – not the kind of terror experienced in a moment of immediate danger, but instead a gnawing horror at the realisation that not only was something terrible going to happen, but it was going to happen to somebody close to him. He'd finally got close enough to see the people involved in the situation on what he now knew to be the roof of a car park, and he realised he knew one of the people very well.

It was his worst nightmare. In all the years he'd been doing this, he'd been plagued with the thought that one day he may be shown a future involving somebody he knew, a future he didn't want to see. But he'd always shrugged the thought away. Now it had happened, and he was powerless to do anything. A warning would only result in disbelief and panic. Even if they did believe him, the people involved would be so conscious of their every move they may unwittingly change the outcome for the worse.

And anyway, in reality what did he actually have to tell? Nothing had really changed. He still didn't know the exact location. He still didn't know what was going on, or what the result of the encounter would be. Until he could figure out who the other person was, and what would lead to the evident confrontation on the rooftop, he had to keep what he knew to himself, and wait. It seemed to be the story of his life at the moment, waiting. But it really was the only option. He couldn't change the outcome until he could gather more information. His only possible actions were gathering knowledge and waiting. And hoping, hoping desperately that he would be able to intervene at just the right moment.

Chapter 36

"She's the girl who was here yesterday with her brother," Kyra told her father who was still looking at her blankly. "You know, you saw us in the kitchen. Lauren and Noah were here too?" Still nothing. She looked toward Noah in a silent plea for backup.

"They've just moved here from America. Kyra's doing an assignment with them. I'm going too, so she won't be coming home on her own," he offered.

"Okay, well, I don't see a problem with that. But Noah, you go to Anderson Bay School. Why are you suddenly hanging out with Cranley High students, huh?" He was wagging his eyebrows and twitching his head to the side, and Kyra wondered with alarm if he was having some kind of fit.

"Dad, what's wrong? Are you okay?"

"I'm fine. I was just wondering if it's this new girl that's the attraction for Noah? You know." He nudged Noah's shoulder and winked.

"Dad!" Kyra shouted, as Noah's face turned ruby red. "You're so embarrassing! Noah's helping us with the assignment that's all. It's science."

"Well, you're not kids any more. It's perfectly natural to develop feelings for the opposite sex. Oh, unless you two...," he raised his eyebrows.

"Dad! Stop. Come on, Noah." Kyra pulled him, fast, into the hallway, shouting behind her, "I'll be back by nine." Looking at the clock on her phone, she knew they wouldn't have much time there at this rate. Before she could apologise to Noah about her dad's odd behaviour, Liam appeared from the lounge, wearing the strangest purple skinny jeans she'd ever seen and a flowery shirt like something you'd expect to see on a seventies theme night. With his dark shaggy hair growing fast, and at least two days stubble covering his face, he was starting to resemble Russell Brand.

"Off out, Ky?" he asked, leaning against the wall in front of the door.

"Yes, we are actually, if you don't mind moving."

"Little Miss Popular these days, aren't you?"

"Very funny. You're just jealous that I actually have some friends. Now can you please move?"

"You going too, Noah?" Liam asked, and Noah nodded.

"Is there something you actually want, Liam? Because we're late." Kyra stared at her brother, annoyed now. What was with her family today? Was she the only sane one left?

"Well, I was going to offer you a lift actually, but if you're not up for it, then fine." He started to walk back into the lounge and Kyra grabbed the back of his vest.

"Hey, come back. If you're offering a lift then we're taking." She had no idea what he was after. But Crystal lived in the hills to the North of town, and it would save them a good half hour if they went by car. She wasn't about to miss that opportunity.

The drive only took five minutes. Liam was unusually chatty on the way, enquiring about school and homework. Kyra wondered if he had a new girlfriend, but didn't bother to ask; she wasn't sure she wanted to know. His last girlfriend, Edna, had been weird enough. She'd had blue hair and so many piercings she resembled a human pin cushion. But it was the way she'd skulked around the house in the middle of the night that had made Kyra uneasy. And she'd always looked at Kyra with the weirdest expression, but had never uttered so much as a single word to her. Kyra had been more than a little relieved when Edna had stopped showing up around the house. When she'd asked Liam what had happened to her, he'd replied, "to every season there is a reason." Kyra had been sorry she'd asked.

"Well according to Joanna, it's just up this lane," Liam said, snapping her back to the present, as he took a right hand turn at a sign announcing "Bramley Hill Farm Shop." Joanna was Liam's sat nav. They drove up a steep narrow lane enclosed on either side by hedges. After about half a mile the lane opened out onto a wide driveway leading to the most incredible house Kyra had ever seen. Even Liam was impressed.

"Woah, Ky, you're moving in some pretty impressive circles these days, huh?"

Kyra and Noah climbed out of the car.

"This place is amazing," Kyra said. They stared up at the converted barn before them. It wasn't just the size of the house that was remarkable, although it *was* large; it was the design. Set in the hillside, it was framed with dark wood and blended perfectly into the surroundings, adding charm to the picturesque view, like a secret woodland fairy castle nestled amongst the trees. *Well, a very modern fairy castle*, Kyra thought.

Nearly the whole of the south side of the building was made of glass. "They must have a great view from inside," Noah remarked.

Turning, Kyra could see their small town stretching out below her at the foot of the hill, edged on the far side by the coastline, like pale yellow icing on a cake. The English Channel glistened in the sunlight beyond.

"They must be loaded to live in a place like this. I had no idea," said Noah.

"Me neither," Kyra said, surveying the front garden that stretched way down to the main road at the bottom of the hill, concealed from the road by the high hedges. It was stunning, just like the house, full of old trees and shrubbery and dotted with colourful woodland blooms.

"Okay, I'll get off. What time do you want to be picked up?" Liam asked, leaning out the car window.

Kyra had forgotten he was still there. Biting back a sarcastic response, she replied, "Err, half eight? Cheers, Liam." Well, she might as well make the most of this odd behaviour while it lasted.

"Half eight it is. Catch ya later." And with that he smoothly swung Ladybird (his red Beetle) in an arc and drove off down the lane with a final toot of the horn.

"Hey guys, come on over," Crystal called, emerging from behind the house, closely followed by a grinning Lauren. Calling "hello," Kyra and Noah made their way over.

"Oh my God, your house is impressive."

"I know, isn't it just amazing?" Lauren shrieked. "And their parents are even more amazing, and they bought the whole house for a *painting*. Can you believe it?" Crystal laughed at the puzzled expressions of the two newcomers.

"My dad's an artist," she said by way of explanation. "He believes in exchange of services instead of money. Well, where possible. He has this friend in the UK who's an architect. So when we decided to move here they struck up a deal. He designed this house, and dad did him a painting he's been wanting for, like, forever," she smiled.

"You seriously got this whole house for a painting?" Kyra asked, eyes wide, and Crystal nodded.

"Well, dad had to pay for the materials and stuff. He's a pretty successful artist. And it wasn't just a little painting, it, like, covers one whole wall in this guy's house – and he has a big house."

"Now that's impressive. So what does your mum do?"

"Oh, she runs the farm shop out back. She grows fruit and veggies and then sells them. She keeps chickens too – for the eggs. They've just gone out to dinner with friends, but you might meet them later if you're still here when they get back."

"They are so nice," Lauren added. "You will love them, trust me!"

Crystal led them around the back of the house, pointing out the different crops and greenhouses as they passed, and the enormous hen coop. Even farther up the hill was another converted barn, this one smaller than the house. "That's the shop," Crystal informed them.

Kyra was more than impressed; she was inspired. It seemed like a perfect way to live, growing your own food, swapping services, everyone getting what they needed. They trooped along a path that weaved through a crowd of old oak trees and right to the back door of the house.

"So what are your parents like? They sound pretty cool. Do they, like, *know*?" Kyra asked.

"About the dream riding? Oh yeah, we told them years ago. They're cool with it. They just let us do our thing."

"They *know*?" Lauren asked again, and Crystal nodded. "Wow, you are so lucky. My parents would freak if they found out."

"Well, they're very open-minded but you're right, we're lucky," Crystal replied as she opened the door and stood aside to let them in. The room they stepped into was at one with nature. A vast oak floor stretched before them and all that filled the space was a large brown leather corner settee, colourful cushions scattered around the floor, and about a million potted plants lining the walls. It resembled an indoor jungle, but the space was so large the room didn't feel crowded by the plants.

"Mum kinda loves plants. They emit positive energy you know, energy we can absorb. It helps us in different ways," Crystal explained.

"That's fantastic! Your parents are really are cool," Lauren said, looking around.

Kyra gasped when she saw the view from the glass wall. It was just as spectacular as she'd guessed it would be.

"Hey, guys," Ray said, entering the room behind them. Kyra noticed that he looked toward Lauren first and held her gaze as she smiled back, a far cry from the previous day when he hadn't made eye contact with anyone. She smiled to herself, pleased for her friend. After saying their hellos, they all settled themselves on cushions.

"So, where do we go from here?" Crystal asked.

"I've been thinking about what Nana Anna said, and wondering if it's some kind of warning," Kyra suggested. By now she'd summarised the early morning conversation briefly to Noah as well as to the others at lunchtime. Pulling the notebook from her bag, she read out the notes she'd taken of her grandmother's visit, in case there was anything of importance she'd missed.

"You might be right, Ky – it could be a warning. Maybe Marco's about to go out and do something stupid again – I think you guys need to find him quickly," Noah said, looking serious. "His behaviour's pretty dangerous. But there's no point speculating until we have more information. I say get over there and see what's going on."

"And leave you alone again, Noah?" Kyra asked, feeling awkward about him constantly being left out.

"Oh, don't worry about me. I have plenty to keep me busy." He pulled a laptop from his rucksack. It was one he'd put together himself, using parts from several broken ones Kyra's father had collected from work over time. "Last night I started typing up a record of everything that's happened so far. Thought it might come in useful some day to have everything documented. I fell asleep before I could finish, though. So I'll just carry on with that."

"Great idea, Noah." Lauren looked impressed. "Kind of like a group diary!"

"Yep, and I want to see if I can find out anything more about those shadows too."

Kyra shivered as she remembered the way the website had vanished after Noah had enquired about them. She'd already filled the others in on that too.

"Well just be careful okay? And we'll check back every now and again to let you know what's happening. Right?" She looked at the others and received nods all round. Noah smiled.

"Okay guys – let's go find Marco!" Crystal rallied and clapped her hands.

Chapter 37

After finding comfortable positions on the carpet, they all lay with closed eyes. Within seconds they were out of their physical bodies, floating in the den. Kyra was astounded by how easy it had become to dream Ride at will in such a short space of time. Switching to telepathic communication as naturally as she breathed, she asked, "Everyone ready?" To which she received three nods. "Good, then let's go."

They found themselves in the spacious upstairs hallway of a house. There was cheery yellow wallpaper, blue carpeted stairs leading down directly ahead of them, five closed doors. Not many visual clues, but Kyra drew the only logical conclusion: Marco's house. They hadn't even time to contemplate their next move before the sound of a flushing toilet came from the end of the hallway, followed by a door opening. Marco emerged and walked down the stairs. The Dream Riders followed, wordlessly agreeing to watch him for a while and try to figure out their purpose here.

Turning right at the foot of the stairs, Marco walked through a large bright kitchen and into a dining room beyond. A man was already seated at the table silently eating a plate of what was just about recognisable as chicken nuggets and chips. He didn't look up when Marco walked in.

"Looks like somebody's been outsourcing their catering to the local crematorium," Ray commented wryly.

The man they could only assume to be Marco's father looked as if he was in his mid-forties, although it was entirely possible he was younger. He was such a mess it really was hard to tell. Wearing a plain blue work shirt that stretched tightly across his rounded gut, with grey stubble foresting flabby cheeks and a double chin, he could definitely do with both a personal trainer and a stylist. Dark smudges beneath the eyes, not just bags but serious suitcases, told a story of many sleepless nights, and deeply etched lines hinted at a hard life. His eyes seemed devoid of colour, grey, lifeless. At first glance they appeared to be fixed on a spot on the dining table, but they were, in fact, looking right through it.

Marco sat down in the chair next to his father's, and picked up his fork. He poked at his food, spearing a chip, but didn't move it to his mouth. Instead he inspected it from every angle, as if it were the most fascinating thing he'd seen.

Kyra studied the room. It was bright and chirpy, but something didn't fit. Up close it was evident the wallpaper was fading, cobwebs streaked the corners of the room, and dust had gathered atop the sideboard. It was more than simple neglect of housework that caused the feeling of "wrongness," though. The atmosphere in the room was so starkly in contrast with the sunny design of the house, it was quite disturbing.

"Can you feel that?" Crystal asked. "It's like somebody sucked all the life out of the house."

Kyra knew exactly what she meant. It was a perfect description of the emptiness that filled the house. This place was a hollow shell, nice carpets and wallpaper masquerading as a home. Not sure what else to do, the group remained in the archway between rooms, watching the silent diners. Kyra felt unsettled, like something was brewing. Whether it was in the room, or in their own lives, she wasn't sure, but a sense of heaviness had descended.

"Do you want some ketchup?" Marco asked his father, slicing the silence with his sudden words. The normality of his question failed to hide the strain in his voice, a fight between hope and anxiety.

The hand he had extended with the offered bottle remained still for what seemed like minutes, despite the complete lack of response from his father. The man didn't even acknowledge the question, just continued to fork chips into his mouth, his dead eyes never moving.

The Dream Riders watched in shock, with nothing to do but continue to observe this uneasy scene. It took a moment for them to notice the tears sliding down Marco's cheeks. He finally seemed to remember his hand was still holding out the bottle and lowered it to the table. His crying was audible now. Snot trailed from his nose.

"My God," Lauren said silently.

Kyra could barely believe her eyes. This was the boy who had tortured Noah and countless others for years? Right now all she could do was feel deep sorrow for hm. It was the last thing she'd expected to see here tonight.

Completely ignoring his son's distress, the man finished the last of his food, took the can of beer that had been sitting near his right hand, and left the room. Marco pushed his plate away and dropped his head into his arms in front of him.

"Sorry, mum," Crystal said quietly.

"Huh?" Kyra asked.

"That's what he's thinking. 'I'm so sorry, mum.'"

Chapter 38

Back in the Hudson house den, the mood was sombre as they described the scene to Noah.

"That's what Nana Anna wanted you to see," Noah said. "She wanted us to understand how unhappy Marco is."

"But why?" Kyra asked, shifting herself to sit on a large green cushion patterned with shiny gold leaves.

"That's what we have to work out, I guess. I think we should start by finding out what happened to his mum, what he's sorry for. Then maybe we'll be closer to figuring out what we're supposed to do."

"Do you think Marco could be our first mission?" Lauren asked as if they were secret agents.

Kyra couldn't help but smile.

"In many ways he might well be, Lauren," Noah replied.

"You're right," Crystal agreed. "It makes sense. After all, nothing is a coincidence."

"Okay, so for a husband and son to be as unhappy as we witnessed tonight, I'd say she either left them, or she's dead," Kyra reasoned. It was logical. Amongst their group they had experience of both scenarios and knew well the pain either could cause. "So how do we find out which of those it is? Noah, can we find out online?"

"Well, yeah, probably, with a bit of digging. But we have an easier method to find out what happened." He looked at Lauren.

"What? Why are you looking at me? Am I supposed to guess the easier method? Do I get three tries?" She put her hand to her chest dramatically.

"No, Lauren, you *are* the easier method. You can go back to Marco's house and memory travel, find out what happened to his mum, to them all."

"Oh," Lauren said. "But doesn't Marco have to actually be thinking about the memory for me to do it? That could be a bit hit and miss."

"Nope, not at all. Remember what I said about places holding memories, as well as people? Memories are just energy like everything else. And something that had such a profound effect on a family is bound to have imprinted its energy as a memory on the house. It should be easy to tune into it."

"Easy for you to say," Lauren laughed nervously. "Do you really think I can do that?" She looked half excited and half terrified.

"All you can do is try. But I have every faith that you will do it. You've been given your tool for a reason Lauren, now's the time to use it."

Kyra gave her friend an encouraging smile. She agreed with Noah, it made sense. And she was glad once again they had somebody in their group who could think so logically and fit all the pieces together. Things had suddenly turned serious, and the pressure to get it right was immense. But first they had to work out what "*it*" was.

"You want a drink or something before we go?" Crystal asked. "I'm kinda thirsty."

"Thanks Crys, but I think I just want to go and get on with it." Lauren let out a small laugh. "I'm pretty nervous," she admitted.

Kyra reached out and squeezed her arm. "You'll be fine, Lauren. No pressure."

"You know what? You don't need us all to come with you if you'd be more comfortable alone. Or...or I could just go with you if you'd prefer," Ray asked softly from his spot at Lauren's side.

"Really?" she asked, and he answered with a smile. "I'd like that. Thanks."

The others tactfully left the room, heading to the kitchen for drinks and snacks. On her way out, Kyra looked back and noticed Lauren and Ray's hands discreetly linked together as they lay side by side, preparing to dream ride.

Chapter 39

For the first time since all this had started, her actions suddenly seemed important, instead of just being a laugh. They were working on the basis that they were meant to help Marco and his father in some way, and she was the one who had the task of finding out why. Right now it was all up to her. She was so nervous about not letting the group down that there was no room left for her to be nervous about Ray.

She liked him way more than she'd ever liked any other boy. She hadn't even admitted to Kyra how long she'd lain awake in bed thinking about him the night before. Eventually she'd given in to temptation and flown into the night to visit him, telling herself he'd be asleep and wouldn't notice her anyway. He hadn't been asleep. He'd been soaring through the hills behind his house. He hadn't been surprised to see her either, but had simply greeted her with a smile as if they'd arranged the meeting in advance.

Their flight through the moonlit hills had been magical, a secret world that was all theirs to explore and enjoy. But even then they'd been playful, testing the waters. This was different. It was as if the intensity of the situation had caused their relationship to suddenly leap a stage, from casual flirting to really caring about each other. As Ray's warm hand enclosed hers, the tingle that set her skin alight transcended the physical. As they travelled the time tunnel, their hands still linked, their energy connected, the tingle magnified.

She felt his encouragement like an inner strength, her own to use, empowering. When they arrived once again inside the DiCarmello house, she was determined she would succeed in her task.

"You okay?" Ray asked, and something in her fluttered. She nodded. "Take it slowly. We'll just move through the house 'til you pick something up. No pressure, just relax."

And so they did. They moved from room to room slowly, silently. Through the dining room, still empty, two plates sitting forlornly on the table, one empty, and one untouched. She found it surprisingly simple to switch on her memory sensor. It was like flexing a muscle. The memory that assaulted her, however, wasn't the houses, it was her own. It was the memory of a father and son living in the same house, but occupying different lives, completely lost to each other. It was the memory of Marco's heart-breaking tears.

Quickly they moved through the kitchen, with a pile of dishes at least three days old stacked high by the sink. Nothing hit her there. They went upstairs and through the first door they came to, the one straight ahead of them, which turned out to be Marco's parents' room. The room had lost its feminine touch. The floral bedcovers looked grubby and emitted an unpleasant odour of stale sweat and a million tears. A beautiful glass vase stood empty and lonely on the windowsill. Like the rest of the house, this room had obviously once been homey, but had faded, its once bright character lost.

Then everything faded, before rushing to life with colours from another time, and Lauren suddenly witnessed a movie of memories. First she saw a couple dancing around the room, laughing at a secret shared joke, a ghost of Motown music guiding their steps. He was the man from the dining room, but in this memory he looked how he was supposed to look, younger, smiling, whole. She was a petite woman with laughter in her eyes and a tangle of black curls dancing to their own beat. Marco's mother, Lauren assumed.

And then the scene switched. Lauren could see the same couple, but sitting on the bed, the woman's head resting on the headboard. Tears flowed freely, but they were tears of happiness, tears of joy.

Marco's mother cradled a new-born baby in her arms and her husband watched with glistening eyes – love and pride pouring from his gaze. "He's us," Marco's father whispered. "He is our love, all poured into this little person." And then he planted a tender kiss on his sleeping son's forehead as the scene switched again.

Lauren tried to will the time period forward – to bring the memories she was seeing to the point where they needed to be, to the part she was half dreading. But the memories she travelled to seemed to be pre-chosen, out of her control, and she had no choice but to accept that she was seeing them for a reason. So she tried to remain vigilant but detached, to take in the details without becoming emotionally overwhelmed.

Sleeping, the couple she saw before her in the next memory were nothing more than a lump beneath the covers. Then suddenly, in through the bedroom door flew a little boy, all black hair and red pyjamas, a whirlwind of energy. "It's Christmas!" he shouted, leaping onto his parent's bed.

A head of dark curls arose from the pillow and a voice croaked, "But sweetie it's only four in the morning."

"Mummy, I'm so excited. I can't sleep," the younger Marco insisted.

"But baby, what if Father Christmas hasn't finished yet? We don't want to disturb him, do we? You wanna sleep in here with us?"

His little head nodded and he clambered beneath the covers, right between his parents. His father's arm reached out and encircled his small body. His mother mirrored the embrace.

It was almost too much for Lauren to watch. How could so much love have just gone – leaving only emptiness? What happened here? She willed herself back to the present and there was Ray, right where she'd left him, right by her side. His tender look of encouragement gave her all the strength she needed to continue.

"Anything?" he asked and she shook her head.

"Just a normal family, lots of happy memories. Come on, let's try another room."

The next room in the hallway appeared to be an unused spare and revealed nothing much at all. The third room along was Marco's, and in the present time he was lying on his bed in the dark, staring at the ceiling. It felt invasive to be in his personal space, but Lauren felt something hit her immediately, and signalled to Ray to wait. She felt the shift as the room morphed before her.

The blue of the walls remained the same, as did the furniture, but the boy sitting on the bed, playing on a Gameboy, was definitely a few years younger than the present day Marco, about ten years old in Lauren's estimation. She sensed in a way she couldn't even begin to explain that this was an important memory and tried to absorb every detail. The curtains were open, revealing a dark night sky beyond, jewelled with thousands of twinkling stars. The glass of the window was edged with snow, and an intricate pattern of frost had webbed itself around the corners. The bedroom was tidy, much tidier than in the present day.

At the sound of footsteps outside the door, Marco leapt under the covers and was giving a very believable performance of a sleeping child by the time his mother entered.

"I know you're not asleep," she whispered. And a grin spread across his face but his eyes remained closed. "Because there is no boy on Earth who can possibly be asleep by eight thirty on the night before their tenth birthday." She approached his bed quietly, and knelt on the floor beside him, so that when he finally opened his eyes he jumped, and they both giggled.

"I thought if I was awake I might not get my presents tomorrow," he said, sitting up.

"And what presents might they be?" she teased, tucking a wayward strand of curly hair behind her ear. "Who said you were getting any presents?"

"Mu-um, I know you've got me the X-Box 360," he said, his eyes alight with the kind of excitement only a child can feel. A flicker crossed her face, almost imperceptible.

"Marco," she said, grinning again. "You asked for a PlayStation. Stop trying to catch me out."

"Haha, mum, very funny. I told you Peter Spinners said the

PlayStation is rubbish. I'm not falling for that."

She paused for a second too long.

"Well who says you're getting anything, young man? I think you're way too old for presents now," she said with a smile, but Lauren could see her mind was elsewhere, distracted. "Come on, bed now, or we'll have to cancel the whole birthday."

He climbed beneath the covers and she tucked him in, giving him a peck on the cheek. "I love you, precious," she said.

"Love you mum," he replied as she turned off the light and closed the door.

Lauren followed her hurried steps along the hallway, down the stairs, and into the lounge where her husband was waiting, two glasses of wine on the coffee table in front of him.

He picked one up and held it out to her. "Thought we should celebrate the last night of our son's ninth year," he said with a smile.

Lauren looked around her. The room was full of Christmas decorations. A tree filled one corner, multicoloured fairy lights twinkling.

"I got him the wrong flippin' games console," she said, taking a swig of the wine. "Apparently he wanted the X-Box 360. Typical. And I was really proud of myself for sorting it out as well." She rolled her eyes. She didn't sound annoyed, just disappointed in herself for getting it wrong.

"Oh, don't tell me you got the PlayStation?" he asked, and she nodded.

"I got it this morning. It's all wrapped already. Do you think it really matters? They're all the same aren't they?" she asked hopefully. "It'll be something else he wants next month."

"But it's his tenth birthday, Love. He's really set on the X-Box." He looked at his watch. "You know it's late night opening tonight. I could get to the shop just in time," he said.

"Are you serious? You can't go out to the shop now."

"I have to, Honey. Can you imagine the look on his face when he opens that PlayStation? It'll only take twenty minutes, there and back." He was standing now, looking for his car keys.

She glanced at the bottle. "You've been drinking already, Luca. I'll go," she said with a sigh.

"Are you sure, Maria?" he asked and she nodded. He kissed her on the cheek before sitting back down again.

"Thanks, love. It'll be worth it in the morning. You'd better hurry, only fifteen minutes until the shop shuts."

Maria walked out the door, shrugging herself into a winter coat. "Save some of that wine for me, won't you?" she called as she closed the door behind her, and he turned his attention back to the soap opera he was watching on T.V.

Lauren glided through the front door into the icy night beyond. She saw Marco's mother walking away down the path. But the memory vanished before she reached the end, and she disappeared into thin air. Retreating back inside, Lauren could tell time had shifted again, but not far. She was in a different memory, and a knock at the door behind her brought Marco's father from the lounge. He opened the front door to reveal two sombre looking police officers.

"Mr. DiCarmello?" one of them asked and Marco's father nodded, his hand going to his mouth as if he knew what was coming.

"Sir, I'm very sorry to inform you there's been a terrible accident."

Chapter 40

"It was on Miller Road bridge. She hit a patch of black ice and the car went over the edge into the river, the barrier broke. Apparently she died instantly from head injuries. That's something, at least..." Noah put the laptop down on the floor in front of him and a bleak silence filled the room.

Ray and Lauren shared the sofa, and he sat with his arm protectively around her shoulders as she shed silent tears onto his chest. It had been a lot for her to see and had left her visibly drained. Kyra was so proud of her friend, and what she'd achieved, and so happy to see the closeness she was developing with Ray. In normal circumstances it would call for much teasing, but these were far from normal circumstances.

"It must be so hard to cope with death...if you think it's the end," Kyra said eventually, hugging a cushion to her chest. It was unimaginable, and for the first time ever she realised how truly blessed she was to have been given the gift of understanding. She'd never needed to fear death or miss those who left the Earth dimension, as she'd always understood the continued existence of the human soul. How raw the pain must be, to honestly believe you will never see a loved one again, never feel them. She felt hollow inside just trying to imagine the anguish, and more than ever she longed to see her Golden Boy again, to feel connected to him.

"Maybe that's it," Crystal said softly. "Maybe we can somehow help Marco and his father to understand it's not the end...take away some of their pain. Do you think that's what this is all about?"

"Could be...how are we supposed to know? What do we do now with the information we have?" Noah asked. For once he didn't have the answers.

"I guess we see what our instinct tells us. We need to take time to absorb what we've learned and see what we feel guided to do," Crystal said, as the beep of a car horn outside punctuated her suggestion.

"That'll be my mum," Lauren said, jumping up and wiping her red rimmed eyes. Ray walked to the window and confirmed her assumption, just as Liam pulled up in the driveway in Ladybird. Ray squeezed Lauren's shoulder and the others gathered their bags.

"Let's sleep on it," Noah suggested. "And talk tomorrow, okay?"

They all agreed.

The drive home was quieter than the journey there had been, and after Liam had gone into the house, Kyra hung back to talk to Noah outside.

"You want to sleep at ours?" she asked. But he shook his head.

"There's nothing for me to be scared of any more, Ky. I need to be at home." They smiled, and she gave his hand a squeeze, realising he had a lot to think about. They'd seen Marco from a completely different viewpoint tonight, and they all needed time alone to reflect. But Kyra guessed Noah had other things ponder too, that reading about Marco's mother's death may have stirred his own feelings, with the accident being so similar to his father's.

"Meet me out here in the morning?" she asked as she unlocked her front door, and he nodded before walking into his own house.

Chapter 41

Deep down Lauren already knew she'd go back that night. The act of getting ready for bed and settling down to sleep was really little more than pretence, to her parents, to herself. The prospect of sleeping seemed crazy. There was just too much still to learn. How had his mother's death turned Marco from a sweet little boy into the bully they knew and loathed? How could they help heal him?

And anyway, tiredness seemed like an alien concept right now. Every cell of her body was wide awake, alert, despite spending half the previous night Dream Riding with Ray. She wondered if Dream Riding actually helped to revive the physical body and made a mental note to ask Noah. Maybe access to all that higher energy had a rejuvenating effect, she thought to herself with a laugh; it sounded like an advert for a new shampoo.

Turning onto her side in her double bed so she was facing away from the door, she pulled the covers up around her head, ensuring her sleep looked as natural as possible should her parents come in to check on her. And then she lifted up effortlessly from her body, into the starlit room.

"Cute pyjamas," Ray said from the corner.

She could have cried with relief at the sight of him. She hadn't relished the prospect of going back to Marco's alone. She looked down at her blue satin pyjamas and wondered if clothes had a higher energy too – if that was how they remained in place during Dream Riding. Another question for Noah.

Ray glowed in the dimness of the room, a star all of her own, her guiding light. She smiled. "You knew I'd go back?"

He nodded. "There was still more there for you to watch. I could see it in your eyes. I didn't want you to go alone, Lauren. I'd have waited here all night if I had to."

She liked it when he said her name. She liked the way he felt so right by her side.

"I didn't want to go alone either. I'm so glad you came." She moved to the window and looked out into the darkness. "You're right, there was more. I just couldn't face it then, it was too much. But I need to see what happened next. Maybe we'll know what to do then."

She felt him softly touch her arms. "You ready?" he asked. She nodded and his hand slipped into hers.

Chapter 42

It didn't take long for Kyra to figure out why she felt so guilty. They'd been nasty to somebody and she'd enjoyed it, simple as that. She'd sought revenge for her own personal satisfaction, without even stopping to consider what caused Marco to behave the way he did in the first place.

Tossing and turning in her bed, she knew sleep would be impossible. Visions of Marco's face filled her head, his terrified expression as they taunted him cruelly on the bridge. Even trying to convince herself they'd only done it for Noah's benefit didn't help. There were other ways they could have tried, ways that didn't scare the life out of him. Maybe all he needed was a friend, somebody he could talk to. In all these years had anybody tried, really tried to befriend him?

And what now? How could they help him? The temptation to call on Nana Anna was strong, but she resisted. They needed to work this one out for themselves. Almost without realising she was doing it, Kyra lifted off into the night, on the chance, the smallest chance, that she wasn't the only one having trouble sleeping. She thought of Lauren first, and focussed on her friends face, assuming she would arrive in Lauren's very pink bedroom. She was taken aback when she found herself instead in the darkness of a lounge she didn't recognise, with Ray at her side. "Hi, Ray," she said, surprised.

"Kyra. Hi. Guess we all had the same idea," he smiled. "Looking for Lauren?"

"Yes, actually, I was hoping I wasn't the only insomniac."

He smiled again knowingly. "The longer you Dream Ride, the less sleep you seem to need. I can only manage a couple of hours a night now and then I'm wide awake. It's annoying sometimes, when you've got nothing to do – but kinda neat when you've got a school assignment due."

"Wow, that's pretty cool."

"Lauren's here too, well, sorta..."

"Memory travelling?" Kyra guessed and he nodded. "So we're in Marco's house?" she asked. Earlier she'd only seen the hallway, kitchen, and dining room. Ray nodded his head and pointed behind her. Turning, she could see Marco's father sitting in an armchair, a newspaper open in his lap, a beer can in his hand.

"Hey guys, great minds think alike," Crystal said, materialising at their side. "Something told me you'd be here," she smiled.

"Hey, sis. So what's your story?" Ray asked.

"I felt pretty bad actually, thinking about Marco and what we did to him with the eggs, you know?"

Kyra nodded in response. She did know.

Suddenly, Lauren appeared and did a double take when she saw all her friends surrounding her. "Wow, a welcoming committee!" she exclaimed. "What are you all doing here?"

"Making things right," Crystal said.

"This is a team sport, Miss Lockett, which requires equal participation from all team members," Kyra imitated Mr. Rogers their P.E. teacher when he'd found them gossiping on the sidelines of a hockey match.

Lauren laughed. "Thanks Ky. Thanks guys. I needed cheering up – this is dismal!" she said, and went on to describe the memories she'd just returned from. "Marco overheard the conversation his father had with the police on the night his mum died. They thought he was asleep upstairs but he wasn't. He was listening at the door.

He heard how his mum had gone out because of him. He heard how she was rushing to get to the shop in time. He heard everything." Tears crept down Lauren's cheeks, and as she listened, hot tears stung Kyra's eyes too. "His father barely spoke to him from that day forward. He barely spoke to anyone. Marco blamed himself for her death, probably still does. He thinks he killed his mother."

"But that's stupid – he was just a kid. We all whine for things now and again. It doesn't mean he's to blame," Kyra said, wondering how somebody could live with that kind of guilt, even if it was self imposed and misplaced.

"You're right, Ky. But if only you could see how it was, he needed somebody to comfort him and explain it wasn't his fault. But there was nobody. Nobody but his father, and he was so lost in his own grief he was incapable of consoling anyone."

"Poor kid," Ray said shaking his head.

"It's worse still. What I came to realise when I looked in Marco's eyes as he followed his father round like a lost puppy, seeking forgiveness, was heartbreaking. Even worse than holding himself to blame for her death is the fact that he thinks his father blames him too."

A blue glow suddenly flickered across the room as Marco's father switched on the T.V. with the remote control, casting dancing shadows in every crevice. One shadow, however, emerged from a corner and didn't seem to obey the natural laws of light and dark, moving with a mind of its own. Like the shapes in the museum, Kyra thought, and a glance at the others confirmed they'd seen it too. The sinister shape moved around them in a circle and then multiplied, growing denser and darker until more smoky shapes broke away and hovered. The draining feeling was still a shock to Kyra, although she should have expected it after last time, robbing her of her energy and her thoughts. This time she didn't even have time to call for help. The shapes were gone almost as quickly as they'd appeared, and she was left wondering if it had been nothing more than an illusion.

Chapter 43

Noah didn't need anyone to tell him that Marco blamed himself for his mother's death; he'd worked that much out for himself. Hell, he'd lived it. Despite the fact he'd not even been born yet and could do nothing to change the tragic event, if Noah hadn't existed, his father would still be alive. He knew his guilt was both ridiculous and pointless, but that knowledge alone didn't diminish it.

He'd never admitted these feelings to his mum. There'd been occasions when he'd watched her getting ready for work, or cleaning the house, that he'd wondered how different her life would have been if she'd never conceived him and her husband had still been alive. Was that how Marco felt every time he looked at his father – sick with guilt and helpless to change anything? The difference was, Marco had known how life was with his mother around. His guilt must be a million times more potent.

The more Noah contemplated it, the more convinced he was that it was he who was supposed to help Marco. After all, it was he who had borne the brunt of Marco's pain for so long, and it was he who shared so much in common with the boy. That was why he turned on his laptop in the middle of the night to find out more, to devise a plan.

At least that's what he told himself. Maybe the real reason was that sitting alone in his house with no fear or dread for the first time in months brought back memories of what they'd done to Marco the previous night. He'd asked his friends to get back at Marco and that was wrong. He'd been lashing out because of his own fear and pain. And when he thought about it, he realised that was exactly what Marco had been doing for years. It was a vicious circle, an endless loop of pain. Somewhere it had to stop. Someone had to break the cycle. Noah was certain, more than he'd ever been certain of anything, that it was his duty to break it.

Chapter 44

The dinner didn't work. Marco had always assumed that when he finally got his dad to sit down and eat with him, it would magically fix things. At the very least, he'd thought it would be an encouraging start and that he'd see some positive changes coming out of it. In reality there'd been nothing. His dad had sat there like a robot, moving only when necessary, and giving no indication that he cared about anything. Giving nothing at all.

Now Marco couldn't even remember why he'd ever thought it might work. The image he'd once held on to, like a beacon leading the way back to normality, the image of a family, a happy family full of laughter and colour as they shared a meal at the end of the day, had crawled far into a dark recess at the back of his mind and was covered with cobwebs, too painful to take out and hold up to the light.

He'd spent so much time focusing on this one goal, he realised there was nothing else. There were no more goals, there was no hope. No hope for him and his father, no hope for respect from his peers. His world had come crashing down last night when that weird shit had happened with the flying eggs. Somehow, Jez and Spam had set him up. They'd taken the piss out of him, and that little bastard Noah was in on it too. The last twenty-four hours had been awful.

Marco hadn't slept all night. He'd been scared out of his wits, and at school he'd been like a recluse. Usually he hoped for attention, craved it, aiming to stand out as much as possible at every moment. But on this day he'd looked pale and withdrawn, and couldn't muster the energy to challenge anyone. He'd spent the whole day obsessing over the previous night's events. How did they do it? Why did they do it? And how many others were in on it? Everyone had turned on him, he just knew it, and now they all thought he was a Muppet. Why, oh why, had he run like a bloody pussy? Screaming like a little girl, he could still hear his own pathetic shriek echoing in his head. He'd trawled YouTube, half expecting to find footage of him legging it from the bridge, convinced it was set up.

Worse still, in desperation he'd come home after school looking for some sort of reassurance from his arsehole of a dad, as if that was ever going to happen. He was sure his father had been deliberately goading him by coming to the table for the first time in four years, raising his hopes just so he would fall even harder. Maybe he was in on it too.

Marco's paranoia and obsessive questioning had driven him to a frantic state. Throughout the day he'd glanced at everyone, cautious, wondering where the next prank would come from. He could see the amusement in all their faces, from the old pisshead in the street to the dinner lady at school. Even a couple of little nerds he'd once pushed around had seemed to sneer at him as he walked past.

But he'd made it to the end of the day with no further episodes. Evidently last night's events hadn't made the school grapevine just yet, although this didn't give Marco any comfort. When he considered it he realised everyone was probably just hiding it from him, sniggering behind his back, and that meant tomorrow it would be even worse. When it all came out it would be unbearable, and at the thought of it Marco's head dropped into his arms as he sat at the kitchen table. He sobbed loudly and uncontrollably, an outpouring of emotion that had been building for over four years, a dam that had been waiting to burst.

The loud sobbing from the hunched figure brought no response from his father sitting in the lounge. Marco was distraught, consumed by dread at the thought of school the next day. He couldn't face it. It was over. And he knew who was to blame. Marco lifted up his head, and used his forearm to wipe the tears from his eyes in one long slow movement.

Standing up, he walked toward the front door. It was suddenly clear in his mind what he had to do. Looking over his shoulder, he shouted, "Bye, dad," expecting no response. And he didn't get one. Slamming the door loudly and striding into the dark rainy night, he said aloud, "You're gonna get what's coming, Noah."

Chapter 45

Lauren was becoming accustomed to the way the memories presented themselves to her, and slipping into them was as easy as saying "yes" in her mind. She'd come to realise she was taken to memories that would help them build up a complete picture of Marco, memories that may seem random and insignificant on the surface but that had in fact shaped the angry, volatile boy they knew today. These memories were like a roadmap to disaster.

She wondered briefly if somebody was guiding her to the right memories, or if it was simply her own intuition. So many questions, but they weren't important now. She would have time to contemplate these details later. Right now, she would just go with it. After the freaky shadowy shapes had disappeared from the room, her friends had faded too, as she'd slipped into another memory.

She now found herself alone in the lounge, the house quiet, sad. Compelled to go into the hallway, she saw Marco stomping down the stairs wearing his school uniform. He didn't look much older than the last memory she'd travelled to, and Lauren guessed that not much time had passed since the accident. Something in Marco's face had definitely changed, however, something in his eyes. They were no longer the eyes of a little boy, innocent and carefree, and she saw none of the hope glimmering there that she'd seen before. Now there was just steely hardness, now all she saw in his eyes was anger.

A knock came from the front door and she watched him pull it open.

"Hi, Marco," a boy muttered, his head bent low. "I'm sorry about what happened to your mum. Are you ready to go?" A second boy stood by his side, averting his gaze with the same awkwardness of a child unprepared to deal with another's grief.

"Piss off you twats. What makes you think I want to walk with you any more? Pair of losers." Marco slammed the door and turned, leaning his back against it. Tears welled in his eyes, and that's when she saw it – that little boy was still there, buried deep beneath the anger.

She returned to her friends and relayed the scene. "He doesn't want anyone to be nice to him. He thinks he doesn't deserve it. He lashes out at everyone around him but it's himself he's really angry with. It's himself he wants to punish."

Chapter 46

He knew it couldn't wait 'til the morning. Something was pushing him to do it now, and of all the things Noah had learned over the past couple of days, the biggest lesson had been to listen to his inner guidance. It only took a few minutes for him to find the address online. He'd considered phoning the house. But it was after ten at night and he didn't want to disturb Marco's father, so he'd decided to go there instead.

He wasn't sure what he'd do when he got there, but had a vague idea of throwing stones at the bedroom window to get Marco's attention. Did people really do that, or did it only work in films? It didn't matter. He just needed to get to the house and he'd take it from there. If he stopped to think about it too much, he'd probably chicken out, and so he pushed aside the images of the taunting and beatings he'd received from Marco in the past. He had to help Marco. It was his duty, and he couldn't afford to turn to jelly now.

As he pulled on his clothes, he tried to work out what he might say to compose his speech.... "Marco, I know you never liked me, but I need to tell you something." Surely that would just earn him a punch in the mouth. "Hi Marco, I know about your mum's accident. I know you blame yourself, and I understand." Way too harsh..."Marco..." Oh ship, this is gonna be a disaster. But Noah slipped on his trainers regardless and searched through the hallway cupboard for his hooded coat, in preparation for the pelting rain. A knock sounded at the front door beside him, and he frowned in confusion. His mum back from work early for some reason? No, she'd have her key. Kyra? Maybe.

Opening the door, Noah gasped with shock. Standing before him in the pouring rain, his saturated hair plastered to his face, his T-shirt and jeans sodden, was Marco. The irony wasn't lost on Noah. He'd spent the last half an hour trying to find him, determined to talk to him, and here he was. But words escaped him, and his heart contracted with fear when he saw Marco's wild eyes, his gaze unyielding, his jaw set in grim determination. A glint caught Noah's eye and he thought he might faint, his trembling legs struggling to support him when he registered the knife in Marco's hand.

"You're coming with me," Marco said forcefully through gritted teeth.

Chapter 47

After Lauren had declared that she wasn't picking up any more memories, that they'd seen all there was to see, it was Kyra who spoke first. "It's not too late," she said with determination, "to befriend him, to show him that he's *worth* being friends with. I know it won't be easy, but if we make a real effort, all of us, he'll have to give in sooner or later. After all, we know all that hard man stuff is an act, a method of self punishment." Okay, so it wasn't much of a plan, as plans go, but it was the best she could come up with on short notice.

"I kind of see what you mean," Lauren agreed. "We could like, badger him into being friends with us. If we make sure one of us is always trying, on the way to school, in class, on lunch break, all we need is for him to listen and then we can get talking about, you know, the accident and stuff, show him that it wasn't his fault."

Ray laughed. "Well, your heart's in the right place, but I'm not so sure it would be *that* easy to just drop it into conversation. Maybe just being nice to him, no matter what he dishes out in return, is enough to chip away the wall of rock he's built up around himself."

"You mean like attacking him with kindness?" Crystal added with a smile. "It'll probably drive him insane! Saying that, I can't think of a better plan. We need to talk to Noah, huh? I bet he'd have a good idea."

It was at that moment, as Crystal mentioned Noah, they heard a muffled voice saying, "Noah's in trouble."

Kyra recognised the voice instantly, but didn't understand. It couldn't be. They all looked around in confusion, not sure from where the voice had come.

"Who was that?" Ray asked, and the voice spoke again, but slightly louder this time.

"Noah is in trouble," it said, and this time a figure appeared.

"Liam?" Kyra asked, her voice spiked with disbelief. Sure enough, there was her brother hovering in front of her. "What the *hell*? You're a Dream Rider?"

"Listen, Ky, there's no time to explain now. Yes, I'm a Dream Rider. I'm also a Visitor – you know what that is?" he asked and she nodded her head, still in shock, vaguely remembering Noah's explanation of Dream Riders visiting the future. "Well I've seen Noah, and he's in trouble. Big trouble. It's happening right now. At this moment I'm in my car on the way there, waiting at a red light, but I'm not gonna make it in time. You have to go find them and do something. Ride there. I've got to go."

"Where is he?" Crystal called after him, ever the cool head. But it was too late. He was gone.

Chapter 48

"Crap!" Liam shouted as he re-entered his body. On the road behind him, which had been completely deserted when he'd stopped in front of the traffic lights, he could now see several pairs of headlights glaring in his rear-view mirror. He'd been aware of the blaring horns while he'd been talking to his sister and her friends, but it had been important to get the message across clearly before coming back.

"Idiot," one driver mouthed as he zoomed past, waving his fist in Liam's direction. Liam started Ladybird's engine and continued on his journey as fast as he dared go in the lashing rain. Dream Riding whilst driving wasn't something he made common practise of, but he'd had no option. The treacherous weather conditions had forced him to keep to a reasonable speed. After all, he'd be no good to anyone dead, and he was still at least ten minutes from the location. And anyway, there'd been no traffic around, and he'd known it would take only seconds to find Kyra, say what he needed to, and get back. He was well practised.

Taking a left turn, Liam decided on the seafront route. Luckily the weather was keeping the roads fairly clear of traffic, and he pressed down a little harder on the accelerator. At last this evening, when he'd visited the event, he'd seen it with the clarity he'd been seeking. He'd seen Noah's terrified expression as he cowered on the roof of the bowling alley car park. He'd seen the other boy too, looking totally out of control, waving a knife wildly as he spoke.

Even if it had been strangers up there, Liam would have done everything within his power to intervene. It was his duty. But seeing Noah, the boy he'd played with and teased over the years and babysat for countless times, the boy he considered to be a little brother, the boy he'd foreseen could do great things to help not just those around him but the whole of humanity, had poured pure dread into his veins. He couldn't fail. He must save him.

With the afternoon being clear and bright, Liam had agreed to sleep at his mum's, assuming the rainy scene in his premonition could not be imminent and therefore it would be safe for him to be a few miles away from Noah for this one night. However, as dark clouds had slowly gathered shortly after dropping Kyra and Noah back home, he'd begun to suspect with growing dread that he was wrong. And so he'd Dream Ridden frequently to Noah's, just to check. And sure enough, the last time, he'd seen him being marched from his house at knifepoint not long after the storm broke.

Visiting the future was a useful tool, but in a situation like this Liam was completely powerless in his energy body. He could do nothing to help Noah without his physical body and so he had leapt from his bed at lightning speed, pulling on his shoes and sprinting into the night, cursing the notoriously unpredictable British weather. He already knew their final destination, and so off he sped, without so much as a word to his mother. Now, as Ladybird sped through the night, he just prayed Kyra and her group had learned enough to save their friend.

Chapter 49

Noah refused to give in to the fear that Marco might seriously hurt, or even kill him. He knew Marco was the one who needed to be saved. He was sure of it. The possibility that he might be wrong was becoming stronger – a thought he'd brushed away often on the drive to town.

Throughout the journey to the bowling alley, Noah had tried to convince Marco of their similarities, of how they could help each other, possibly even befriend each other. It wasn't the scenario he'd envisaged. And it wasn't exactly how he'd imagined the conversation would go when he'd been preparing for it earlier; but the facts were the same nonetheless. He hadn't stopped believing in Marco when he was held at knifepoint on his own doorstep, or when he was thrown into the boot of Mr. DiCarmello's car, which Marco had stolen (probably not for the first time), or as he was dragged up the stairs of the multi-story car park. He'd continued to try and talk to an unresponsive Marco the whole way. But now they'd reached the roof of the car park, Noah started to waver in the certainty that he could appeal to Marco's better side.

"Look Marco, what are we doing here?" he asked, his words almost lost in the howling wind. "You don't have to do this, you know."

Marco was looking less in control of himself than he was of the situation. He put his hands on his head whilst still clutching the knife, a look of utter frustration twisting his face. "Shut up, you stupid idiot. I kept telling you to shut up in the car, and you just kept shouting through the boot, didn't you?" He looked directly at Noah, and walked toward him, his hands still on his head. "You kept shouting over and over 'I can help you, it doesn't have to be this way, I understand, we're the same you and me.' All that CRAP." Grabbing Noah's collar, Marco marched him toward the edge of the roof, five stories above the road below. "You can't help me. No one can. You think you've got a clue how I feel? No chance, mate."

They were now just a couple of feet away from the low barrier that bordered the edge. The height, mixed with the driving rain, the regular clashes of thunder, the flashing lightning, and Marco's rage, finally caused Noah to give in to the terror of the situation. He fell to his hands and knees, not wanting to see the dizzying panorama. Looking up at Marco pleadingly, he said, "Don't do it, Marco. I'm begging you, please just don't. This isn't the way. It's not the answer. I know what happened to you. I know everything."

Marco slowly shook his head as he gazed over the edge and into the black night. "No, it's too late. This is how it's supposed to be. What goes around comes around. We've both got this coming."

"You don't understand. When I told you that I blame myself for my dad's death, I didn't mean that I needed to be punished. I just meant that I can understand how you feel inside. You know, deep inside."

"God, you talk a lot of shit, don't you? You and I both deserve this, don't you see?" Marco now wouldn't even look at Noah. He was focussed entirely on the edge of the roof, and he edged closer still. He stepped over the low barrier as lightning split the sky and thunder rumbled like an angry dragon's warning growl. And with one swift swing he threw his knife high over the edge and into the inky night.

"It was ALL MY FAULT," he shouted. "If I'd never been born, none of this would have happened. If I hadn't been such a greedy little shit, none of this would have happened. And there's no one else to blame. *She* should be here, not me." This last part came out as a pitiful whisper, no anger left in his face by then, or in his voice. All of the rage had simply drained out of him, as if it had blown away in the swirling wind. With one hand holding onto the barrier behind him and both feet now at the very edge of the short ledge, he glanced back at Noah who was still on his knees and said, "An eye for an eye, right?"

"No, not an eye for an eye. That's complete rubbish. You were only a kid. You can't take the blame for this."

Marco let go of the barrier, and there was nothing to secure his safety. Even a strong gust of wind could be enough to topple him over the edge.

"You don't want to do this," Noah said calmly, his voice betraying none of the terror that was gripping his insides. "You want me to talk you out of it. Why else would you have brought me here?"

Marco laughed with superfluous amusement, completely out of place in the situation, a crazy sound. He quickly regained his composure. "Well if I wanted you to talk me out of it, you ain't doing a very good job, are you? No, I wanted you to watch the blood and guts. Because that's what you were after wasn't it? When you pulled that egg stunt – don't deny it." He looked out over the precipice and said quietly to Noah, "To be honest, mate, I just can't take it anymore. I want it to end."

There was no doubt in Noah's mind that this was it. Marco had said his final word, and from his position on the ground it seemed that Marco's body was poised for the leap.

"I wanted an X-Box too you know, when I was ten," he shouted in desperation. He couldn't let this happen. Standing, he could see Marco's posture stiffen.

"You what?" Marco asked slowly and quietly. His hand grabbed the barrier behind him and he swung his head round. "How did you know about the X-Box? You been talking to my old man?"

Noah's heart sunk. He'd spoken without thinking, in desperation, and he didn't know how to explain it in a way Marco would believe. His mind went blank. "I can't tell you how I know," he muttered.

And as Marco shook his head in dismissal and turned back toward the stormy night, his silhouette small against a flash of lightning beyond, Noah knew he'd lost his big chance, his only opportunity.

But then Noah stepped slowly toward the edge so he was standing right at the barrier to Marco's left, and in a calm clear voice he said, "He's thinking about you right now, you know. And her. He's replaying the conversation with the police over and over again as we speak; the conversation you heard through the lounge door. He hates looking you in the eye because he can't bear the guilt he feels when he remembers that he took her away from you. He's sure the accident was his fault and no-one else's. Your father blames himself for her death, just like you blame yourself."

Chapter 50

Sweat dripped from his brow as Liam pushed Ladybird to her limit. He'd already been flashed by one speed camera, and he'd skidded on the wet roads numerous times. But that didn't matter to him. All that mattered was getting there. As he came around the last corner he realised how close he was, close enough to see the car park, close enough even to just make out the two figures standing perilously close to the edge of the roof level.

Forcing the accelerator to the floor, he expected to hear Ladybird growling in her efforts to propel him along the road, but instead he heard her cough and splutter and she actually decreased in velocity. Stunned, he glanced at the fuel gage. Nothing. Nada. He was running on empty.

Bugger, it's too late. I'm never going to get there in time he thought, and slammed his fists down on the steering wheel when the car had chugged to a stop. But he couldn't stop trying, he couldn't just give up. Unbuckling himself he threw open the door and sprinted into the pouring rain.

Chapter 51

"Show him the police, show him the police," Lauren shouted at Crystal.

"I already have," Crystal replied impatiently, her voice rising, her calm demeanour showing cracks under the mounting pressure of the situation.

"What about the things you saw in his dad's head when he was watching *Eastenders*?" Lauren suggested. They were all desperate to give Noah something that would stop Marco from jumping.

As Lauren and Crystal continued their exchange, Noah spoke again, his voice calm and steady. "Did you know he doesn't even like *Eastenders*? Or any other soap. He only ever sits there staring to try and hide from you, always trying to avoid your gaze, just in case you realise that he's to blame."

Kyra was so proud that Noah had got it. She'd been terrified he wouldn't realise they were there, wouldn't understand the images Crystal was putting in his head, but he'd got it immediately. He'd even stood up and started walking confidently while relaying what he was being shown.

"Look, just STOP!" Marco shouted, his head still turned toward Noah, and lifted his hands to his ears. The action, and the confusion of the moment, unbalanced him and he teetered unsteadily, precariously. They could all see the terror etched in Marco's face as he realised he was going to fall. Noah reached out in an attempt to grab Marco's trailing arm, but it was no use. He was too far away. It seemed to happen in slow motion. Although Marco's feet were still on the ledge, his body was leaning too far forward for him to regain his balance.

"Oh my God, he's falling!" Lauren screamed.

Chapter 52

It was as Marco started to fall that he realised with a sudden clarity that he didn't want to die. But the windmill action of his arms made no difference at all, and he stared in horror into the gloomy street below, watching the fat drops of rain as they fell away from him into the darkness, shimmering streaks, confident in their plunge to the concrete. He noticed how small all the cars were. Thoughts rushed through his mind in that instant, and he even had time to wonder how long it would take before those cars below became a whole lot bigger as they rushed up to meet him.

His toes were still on the ledge. Time was moving so slowly it seemed to be standing still, but the street below appeared to come no closer. He didn't expect it to take this long. With his body suspended at a forty-five degree angle, he at last noticed the pressure he felt on his chest.

Confused, he looked around him, bent his head to his chest in an attempt to see what was holding him. Nothing, there was nothing there, but somehow, inexplicably, he felt himself being pushed upward, higher and higher until he was nearly standing straight again. And then with a sudden burst of pressure he went flying backward, the back of his thighs hitting the barrier behind him, and he landed in a deep puddle on the tarmac.

Breathing heavily, his heart hammered in his chest as if trying to escape its bony cage. Words failed him as relief and adrenaline coursed through his veins and tears sprang to his eyes. "What? What the hell... " was all he managed to utter.

"It's okay, Marco. You weren't supposed to die tonight," Noah said gently, and walked to his side. He sat beside him, not caring about the wet ground; they were drenched from the rain anyway. "Look Marco, I don't know how to tell you this but you were just saved by a Dream Rider. My friends are Dream Riders."

"Dream what?" Marco asked, looking perplexed.

Chapter 53

"Now that was truly spectacular!" Lauren gushed. "You were... just...just...awesome! How did you do that? You got there so quickly."

"Lauren, I don't even know how I did it," Ray shook his head, still slightly stunned. "I just knew I couldn't let him fall, not if I wanted to live with myself. I tell you what though – it was scary there for a minute, I had to use my whole body. There was a second when I thought my hands were gonna just go right through him."

"Well done, Ray. Great work," Kyra smiled and Crystal beamed at her brother too. They all turned to watch the pair on the ground below, where Noah was still busy trying to convince Marco of the existence of Dream Riders. Now that the immediate danger was over and she could tell that Marco didn't currently want to kill either himself or Noah, Kyra could admit to herself it was actually quite funny to watch Noah floundering in his attempts to explain.

"So you're saying you're all, like, superheroes?" Marco asked, his eyebrows arched in disbelief.

"Well no, not really... "

"What then? Like MI5 agents?"

"No, look, Marco, when I said we have missions I didn't mean those kinds of missions. We just help people to, to... " Noah looked like he was struggling to find any more words.

"So you go on missions to help people. And your friends can fly, but they're invisible. Which is why you can't prove any of this to me?" Marco asked.

Noah beamed. "Exactly. You got it!"

Kyra squirmed for her friend. Didn't he hear the dripping sarcasm in Marco's voice? She looked around at the others, trying to think of a way to help Noah explain. They all looked as clueless as she. "We need to do something," she said. But nobody answered.

Down below them Marco rolled his eyes. "And I thought I had problems. Never mind helping other people, you should be checking yourself into the local loony bin."

"Okay, well if you don't believe me, how do you explain why you didn't fall?" Noah asked, lifting his chin defiantly. Marco shook his head to indicate he had no explanation.

"I don't know how you did it, and I don't know how you did that thing with the eggs. Maybe you're into some weird voodoo stuff. Maybe it's...I don't know, I don't have a clue. But I don't think I wanna have anything more to do with this. You're a nutter, mate." He got to his feet, rain still slashing furiously onto the ground around him, and started walking slowly back toward the staircase.

"This isn't good," Kyra said. "We can't let him just go, not like this. We need something, something that will make him really believe Noah. Something that will make Marco believe he's not to blame. Otherwise, he'll probably just end up back up here tomorrow, or next week – we might not be able to stop him next time."

"I could keep showing Noah stuff only Marco would know," Crystal suggested.

"I don't know. We've done that. It might just freak him out even more," Kyra said, desperately seeking an idea in her frantic mind.

"How about if Ray, like, writes on the concrete with chalk or something? He couldn't deny that!" Lauren contributed to the very limited pool of ideas. They all looked down at the pellets of rain bouncing on the surface of the ever growing lake on the roof below them. "Okay, stupid idea," Lauren said.

At last an idea struck Kyra. "I think I may have something. I don't know if it will work, but if it does, it could be perfect. "

Chapter 54

Marco was halfway across the roof when Noah finally caught up to him, his trainers splashing in the rainwater, his socks, like the rest of him, completely drenched. He caught hold of Marco's shoulder and pulled until he spun around to face him. Possibly a dangerous move and something he wouldn't have dreamed of doing a few days ago without first planning his own funeral. But he didn't think he was in danger, all the anger seemed to have seeped out of Marco and into the puddles below, for now at least. And anyway, Noah had to stop him; he had to make sure.

"I know it's confusing, Marco. I don't expect you to understand. But please just promise me one thing...promise me you won't top yourself?"

Marco shook his head slowly, seeming to actually give the request some consideration. "I don't think I can make that promise, mate," he said, and turned back, continuing his march across the roof.

Where the hell had the others gone? Noah wondered. After saving Marco from his plunge (a move Noah had been hugely impressed with), his friends seemed to have deserted him, although he knew they wouldn't have done so without a good reason. It was astounding the way they'd all pitched in and used their tools to help, like a proper dream riding group. But now it seemed to be all down to him, and he had no idea what else he could do, what else he could say. Foraging in the depths of his mind, he tried to grasp some words, something, anything, but they slipped from his grip every time he came close. Frantically, he continued to follow Marco; he'd follow him all the way home if he had to, until he could find a way to convince him.

Then suddenly he saw an image in his head, as clear as day. It was a woman, wearing a yellow sundress, black curls framing the serene smile on her face. And he saw words too: "Marco's Mum is here to talk to him," as if they'd been scrawled in chalk on the blackboard of his mind. He didn't know exactly what they planned to do, but he guessed Kyra had somehow mastered her tool. His heart swelled with pride. He could have cried with relief.

"Well, if I can't convince you that you deserve to live, I think there's somebody here who can," he called after Marco, and both boys came to a stop.

"What are you going on about now?" Marco asked. He spun around and Noah saw his mouth gape open, as his gaze fixed on something behind Noah. At the same moment the sky surrounding them lightened; and Noah felt a shiver down his spine, his skin breaking out in goose pimples. Turning to look he sucked in a breath and his hand flew to his mouth.

"Mum?" Marco cried. And sure enough there she was – as beautiful as the picture Crystal had put in Noah's mind. She stood before them in her yellow sundress, untouched by the rain, unmoved by the wind. She was like a vision, but oh so real, made from light yet undeniably there. Glimmering and sparkling like a star in the night.

"Yes, baby," she said. Her voice was magic itself, a whisper, a breeze.

Noah moved to the side, allowing mother and son the moment they needed.

Marco walked slowly toward her, eyes wide, tears flowing. "Are you real?" he asked in a shaky voice and reached out a hand. Mirroring the gesture she touched her fingertips to his and Marco gasped as a golden glow spread through his hand and up his arm.

"I can feel you," he whispered. "It's really you... "

"I'm as real as I ever was, but I'm a spirit now. I'm still with you, always. Your new friends will explain. I'll love you forever, baby. I'll never leave," her silky voice echoed around them, and Marco hung his head.

"Mum, I'm sorry. I'm so sorry, for what I did." The words dropped like stones into the puddles below.

"Look at me, Marco," she said, her voice soft but firm. "You have nothing to be sorry for, nothing. Everything is what it is. I was meant to come home. It was my time. And it's a wonderful place to be. I get to watch you every day. I have nothing but love for you." She shone brighter still, as his eyes met hers, and he cried even harder, years of hurt and guilt melting like warm ice in the rain. He had no words, he needed none; the look that passed between them said it all. Noah felt like an intruder on such special moment and shrunk farther into the background.

"I love you, mum. I miss you so much," he said eventually in a whisper.

"Talk to me sometimes and you'll feel me at your side. You can't miss what you haven't lost. It's not your time to come home yet, Marco. You have more to achieve here. I have to go now, baby, but only in sight."

She wrapped her arms around him then and he closed his eyes and let his head fall against her shoulder. They stayed like that for a long moment, until she eventually pulled back and looked at him. "Before I leave there's one thing I must ask...your father...he hurts so much. But he loves you, you know. He needs you to show him, somehow, some way... " She was fading now, visibly, and Marco nodded his head to show he understood. He was sobbing still, but with joy and relief and emotions that had no name.

"I love you, baby," she said, as she vanished from sight. And as Marco fell to his knees, Noah felt the wet tears on his own face too. He'd witnessed something so wondrous, so magical, he could barely believe...and finally after all these years of searching he knew for sure, there was no more doubt. If Marco's mother was still there, by her son's side, then it followed that Noah's father must be with him too.

Chapter 55

Liam had visited enough futures to know his sister could, and would, do great things, but seeing her in action with his own eyes was something else entirely. He'd finally arrived, soaking and panting, at the top of the car park stairs, just as Marco's mother had appeared. He'd barely even had time to register relief that the boys were both still breathing and in one piece, when she'd emerged, golden, from the stormy night. Liam had seen some staggering things in his time, but that – well – there were no words to describe the sight of the two worlds connecting in that way, the frail veil between dimensions lifted. The energy had been immense, and he'd known immediately it was Kyra's work.

He'd sat on the roof in the shadows of the stairwell and easily lifted out of his body so he could see things from the other side, and the sight before him had been even more stunning than that in the physical dimension. Watched by her awestruck friends, Kyra had hovered, arms flung wide, pure white energy visibly pouring from her every cell flowing into the spirit of the woman. That was how the woman had been able to make herself seen in the physical. Only the energy of a Switcher was powerful enough for that kind of manifestation.

He'd remained quiet, not wanting to break Kyra's concentration, as it was easy to see the strain in her face. So like the others, he'd watched the emotional scene play out below, only speaking when Kyra's energy had eventually flagged and the spirit had left the physical and then disappeared also from the realm of the Dream Riders, leaving behind only declarations of gratitude.

"That's my little sis, you know!" he said, and they all turned to greet him.

"You made it!" cried Lauren.

"Lucky he didn't jump, isn't it? Fat lot of good you'd have been now," gasped Kyra from her position in the corner where she was gradually regaining her energy.

Liam laughed. "What can I say? Ladybird's poorly...and anyway, I had to give you guys a chance to shine, didn't I? Looks like you did a pretty good job without me."

"We managed, I guess," Lauren said with a smile. "With teamwork! Talking of which, Liam....do you belong to a group?"

"You could say I'm a bit of a loner," he said turning to face Lauren. "I join up with groups, now and again, when I need to. But seriously, I have to say, you have all been fantastic tonight. The finest I've ever seen."

"Thank you, Liam. That's nice of you to say so. We're all blessed, although I'm still in shock about what Kyra managed to do. I think we all are," Crystal said. "How long have you been dream riding, Liam?"

"A while, you could say. And I know, Ky, I have a lot of explaining to do, but it'll have to wait. I need to get these boys home." He gestured to the two figures sitting in a stunned silence below, and spun to face the spot where Kyra had been. But it was now just a shadowy corner, empty. Kyra had gone.

"Where's Kyra?" he asked, as they all looked around, bewildered. "I bet she drained herself too much to sustain the Dream Ride. She's probably gone back to her body. Look, I need to go back down there and get these boys home. Will you guys go and check on Ky? Just make sure she's feeling okay."

"Of course we will. Don't worry," Crystal said with a smile. And he had no doubt they would make sure she was fine. Such a tight group, so in sync with each other, and with such a competent range of tools, was rare to find.

Returning to his body, he walked over to where the two boys were now talking quietly and was shocked to even hear laughter as they discussed what had happened. They both looked up as he approached, matching expressions of surprise on their faces, as if they'd forgotten other people existed, other people outside of the strange world they'd entered tonight.

"Liam? What on Earth are you doing here?" Noah asked.

"I've come to take you home. Long story...I'll explain on the way. I'm Liam, Kyra's brother, Noah's friend, and a Dream Rider, by the way," he said in Marco's direction, smiling gently. "I gather it's been quite an eventful night."

"You could say that," Marco said, shaking his head. "I don't think this day could get much weirder...or much better," he laughed. "It's gonna take a while to get my head round all this."

"It will, you're right. But you'll get there. We all do." He held out a hand and pulled Noah to his feet, then, looking at Marco, he said, "I gather you've got some bridges to build at home. Well, we've got quite a journey ahead of us in more ways than one." He laughed, "Oh, and no car, so we'd better get a move on." He offered his hand to Marco.

"You're right about the bridges, but wrong about the car." Marco reached out his own hand and opened his fingers to reveal a shiny set of car keys.

Chapter 56

"Can you believe we, like, just totally saved Marco's life? And saw a dead person, well, you know, a spirit. I mean, how cool was that?" Lauren asked. She'd managed to remain calm throughout the drama but had quickly returned to her usual zealous self as they watched Liam and the two boys walking toward the stairwell. Unable to control herself, she was just bursting with everything that had happened.

"That's *was* pretty cool," Ray agreed, smiling at her affectionately. "Not something you see every day."

"And you were just awesome, Ray. You saved the day again, you were like Superman!" She replayed the mental video she'd stored of Ray diving down from the edge of the car park and throwing his hands up just in time to stop Marco's fall. She'd thought she couldn't possibly be any crazier about him, but she was wrong.

"And Crystal, the way you got Noah to understand those images, wow. I mean, seriously, *wow*. And Kyra, Oh My God, she is just so totally the best, like the Ghost Whisperer. We could get our own T.V. programme – *Dream Riders to the Rescue!* The whole thing was like something out of a science fiction film. But it's real, it's all real. It's unbelievable. But believable, if you know what I mean, and... " She just couldn't translate her thoughts into words fast enough to convey what she was feeling. She'd met the most amazing boy in the world, cool, super good looking, and not scared to admit his feelings. And she'd discovered supernatural powers *and* joined an unbelievable group all in just a few days.

"Hey Lauren," Crystal laughed. "I hate to interrupt, but we really should go check on Kyra, make sure she's feeling okay. Don't you think?"

"Oh My God! Yes, of course. Yes, let's go." *Okay, get a grip girl, calm down,* Lauren instructed herself. She decided to try and take a leaf out of cool-as-a-cucumber Crystal's book and awesome-under-pressure Kyra's, and made a silent resolution to stop acting like a complete skip.

"Okay, so Kyra's room it is!" Crystal said, smiling.

Oh God, she heard me, Lauren thought. Shaking her head, she took a deep breath and linked hands with Ray as they travelled through the tunnel.

When they arrived they found Kyra's bedroom empty, her covers crumpled.

"Oh, she must be in the little girl's room. Bad timing," Lauren smiled. "Maybe we should give her a bit of privacy – come back in a while?" *That's it, calm and grown up, in control.* She praised herself and then quickly looked at Crystal to see if she'd heard. But Crystal was staring into a corner of the room, frowning in concentration.

"Help," Crystal whispered and the others rushed to her side, alarmed. She looked at them, her face screaming concern, and continued, louder now. "Oh no, it's Kyra. She's saying 'help.' I can see it. I know it's her. She's calling to us."

"What do you mean? But she..." Lauren started, confused.

"We need to go to her; the words I see are red. That's not good. It means fear, or danger."

"But how could she be in danger? She was just with us. I don't understand." They'd just saved the day, hadn't they? Everything was fixed now. How could Kyra be in trouble? Lauren's breath grew faster as panic rose.

"It's okay, Lauren. We'll find her," Ray assured her, his voice low and calming, as he took hold of her hand. "Okay?" She nodded.

"Good, now let's all focus on Kyra, and go to her."

Lauren tried, she tried really hard but it was difficult. Despite concentrating hard on Kyra's face, her brown eyes, her shaggy hair tied up in two high pigtails, she remained in Kyra's bedroom. Ray and Crystal wore matching expressions of determination, but Lauren could see they were struggling just as she was. Eventually she felt herself moving, but unlike the usual clarity of colour and light, the tunnel they travelled through was blurry and dim. It took a colossal amount of effort to go anywhere, and took longer than it ever had before. Her movement was laboured, her energy body feeling heavy and dense, and the act of even thinking was draining her beyond belief. What was going on here? This was nothing like the usual experience of Riding.

"I can't, I don't... " Lauren started to say. But her words were gone, lost from her mind before the sentence had even formed. She clung to Ray's hand like a lifeline as fear rose inside her. Finally they emerged, after what seemed like an age, all feeling disorientated and weakened. Lauren was baffled by the experience of the tunnel and by how drained she still felt. But most of all her concern for Kyra was growing, and as she looked around she realised her friend was nowhere to be seen. They were above a motorway, sparse traffic zooming along below. "What...where is she? Why don't I see her? And why did that feel so wrong...so hard?" Lauren asked.

"I don't know. Something's definitely not right. It's that van, see there – that white van. She's in there. I can feel it." Crystal was pointing to a transit van speeding along the nearly deserted road below, and they all began to move above it, regaining their buoyancy at last.

"So let's get in there. Why didn't we come out inside the van?" Lauren asked and focused again on Kyra's face, trying to get closer, to will herself next to her friend. It didn't work – she went nowhere – and could see Ray and Crystal looking as confused as she felt.

"I'm gonna just dive down in there and see what's going on. You stay up here, okay?" Ray said. And without waiting for confirmation he nose-dived at top speed toward the van. When he reached within a few metres of the vehicle, however, he seemed to suddenly stop, and bounced upward as if propelled from an invisible barrier. The force caused him to slow down and lose ground, falling behind them.

"Ray!" shouted Lauren and was immediately at his side. "Are you okay?"

He nodded. "I think so – a bit weak, dizzy. There's something stopping us from getting close. I don't know what it is, but it's not good."

Returning to Crystal's side, they followed the van from a good distance above.

"Oh God, I don't like this. Why is Kyra in that van? And why can't we get to her? Do you think she's been kidnapped?" Lauren asked, distressed, all intentions of remaining calm forgotten.

"I hate to say it, but it looks that way. We need help. Look, I'm gonna go find Liam, tell him what's happened. You guys stay with the van. Whatever you do don't lose it okay? It was hard enough to get to it in the first place." And with that last command, Crystal was gone.

Chapter 57

"I still can't believe you stole your father's car. You're fourteen years old. Weren't you worried about getting caught? Or getting in an accident?" Liam looked over at Marco, who was sitting in the passenger seat.

Marco smiled wryly. "To be honest, mate, I wasn't really thinking about consequences. Where I was planning to go, none of that would have mattered. Whoa, slow down, watch my dad's car okay?" he said, putting a steadying hand on the dashboard as Liam suddenly overtook the car in front.

Liam let out a loud laugh. "I like you. You're funny. So Noah, not got the hang of the Riding thing yet, huh?" He glanced in the rearview mirror as he spoke.

"Well, no," Noah replied from the back seat. "Hold on, what do you mean, *yet*? Does that mean in the future I can Dream Ride?" he asked, leaning forward excitedly.

"Ha, nice try, but I follow the strict Visitor's Code of Conduct – and do not reveal what I've seen unless it's absolutely vital." His eyes met Noah's in the mirror, and he gave him a wink.

"Watch the road!" Marco yelled.

"There's a code of conduct?" Noah asked with surprise.

"Well, there is now. I just made it up," Liam said as he turned off the seafront, heading toward Noah's house. "Right, I'll drop you first, Noah, then get Marco and the car home and walk back from there."

"It's okay, I can come with you, maybe help explain to Marco's dad about the car." Marco laughed and turned toward Noah. "Thanks anyway, mate, but he probably hasn't even noticed it's gone. He don't move from his chair all evening. And when he does it's only to drag himself to bed."

"And anyway," Liam added, "you're soaked, and I'm not going to be responsible for you catching pneumonia. You need a warm bath, a warm drink, and a good night's sleep!"

"Yes sir," Noah laughed at the way Liam had suddenly turned into Mr. Responsible. He was still finding it odd to think that Liam had been Dream Riding all these years. Were there any clues? He wondered if he would notice any hints if he looked back and dissected the many childhood memories he had of his neighbour, Kyra's strange older brother. He honestly thought there weren't. Liam had always been *weird*, but that was just Liam. Noah and Kyra had often joked that it was some kind of genetic defect.

Now he wondered if maybe Liam wasn't weird at all and it had all been a clever disguise.

"I wonder how the others are," he said, thinking of Kyra, and the amazing feat she'd performed. "From what I understand, it can be extremely draining using some of those tools. An immense amount of energy is required for manifesting."

"Impressive, Noah. You're not just a pretty face after all," Liam joked.

"Well, I've done a lot of research. And I know that any Dream Rider who uses density tools has to use a lot of energy to slow down their vibrations sufficiently. I bet Kyra and Ray are really feeling it now. They... " He stopped suddenly as an image filled his head. The blackboard again. He immediately knew it was Crystal and with alarm he read the words she'd spelled out.

"Stop the car!" he shouted, and Liam slammed his foot down on the brake, causing the car behind to do the same.

"Jesus, my dad's car! You're a maniac. You'll get us all killed,"

Marco said, clutching the sides of his seat.

"Well, you've certainly changed your tune," Liam said, as he steered the car to the side of the road, horns screaming out angrily behind them. "What did you see?" he asked, turning to Noah.

"Kyra's in trouble. Crystal's here. You need to talk to her," Noah said, trying to stay calm. *How could Kyra be in trouble? What did Crystal mean?*

"Wait here, back in a sec," Liam said, and leaning his head back against the headrest, he closed his eyes.

"What? What the hell is he doing? Having a kip? He almost smashes up my dad's car and now he's having a kip? Is this guy actually crazy?"

"Well, that's a very real possibility. But, no, he's not sleeping. He's dream riding."

"Really? So he's not there in his body now? He's, like, flying?" Marco looked sceptical. A sudden tap on the window made them all jump. Noah rolled down his window, his heart speeding.

"Everything alright?" asked a middle aged man in a suit, frowning with concern. "It's just that you stopped very suddenly. You could have caused an accident." He was squinting through the front window, looking at Liam.

"Oh yes, we're very sorry," Marco replied, leaning over from the passenger seat. "We had a medical emergency. He's, err, diabetic."

"Oh, gosh." The man pulled a phone from his pocket. "I'll call the emergency services."

"No need for that," said Liam, suddenly opening his eyes. "Emergency sugar supply right here." He held up a packet of Polos. "I'll be right as rain in a minute, but thanks for the concern. Always nice to know there are still some good hearted citizens around."

"Oh, okay, well if you're sure... "

All three occupants of the car nodded and smiled brightly. Looking dubious, the man walked back to his own car.

"That was quick. What's happening?" Noah asked turning back to Liam.

"It's not good, Noah. It's really not good," Liam replied gravely.

Chapter 58

Dismayed, Lauren realised Ray was flagging. She tried boosting her own energy and sending it to him to keep him going, concentrating hard on pouring white light through her hand and into his, up his arm and around his body. She had no idea where this knowledge had come from. But giving light energy felt like a natural act, one that went hand in hand with Dream Riding. They were falling behind the van now, their speed dropping rapidly.

"Lauren, thank you, it's helping, but you have to go on ahead. Kyra needs you. I'm losing it – I can't keep up." He was fading as he spoke. "I think using my tool like that drained me." He slackened his fingers trying to release his hand from hers, but she held on tight.

"Ray, don't let go, I need you... "

"You'll be fine, Lauren. Kyra needs you now. You can't lose that van. I'll be right behind you, I promise. I'll just go back to my body... recuperate...back before you know it."

Lauren looked from the van to Ray and back again, and she knew he was right. She couldn't lose the van. She needed to stay with Kyra so they could find a way to get to her. She opened her mouth to agree but he was already gone. She was alone.

Willing herself above the van, she continued flying, refusing to let fear engulf her. Ray would be fine; he'd been doing this for years.

She needed to do everything she could to make sure Kyra was okay now, and flaking out wasn't going to help anyone. *I'm coming to get you Ky. I promise,* she thought with determination, hoping that somehow Kyra would be able to hear her.

The van travelled only a few more miles and then took an exit from the motorway. Lauren mentally noted the junction, repeating it over and over to ensure she didn't forget. She also memorised town and village names announced on road signs along the way in case she might need to give directions.

The roads the van was choosing became narrower and seemed to be leading them farther into the countryside, leaving behind all other traffic. As the built up areas petered out, so did the man-made lighting, and Lauren moved closer still to the van to ensure she didn't lose sight of it. The rain may have stopped but the clouds hadn't yet completely dispersed, and the moon was hidden from view, leaving an inky black night all around her. As soon as she drew close to the van, she felt an effect like an electric shock, and she gasped, moving quickly away again, continuing at a safe distance from the vehicle.

Just then the van made a left turn into what looked like an industrial estate of some kind, consisting of many large buildings, with vehicles scattered all around. The van passed through grand metal gates, which quickly clanged closed behind it, obviously controlled by some kind of electrical mechanism. There was some light here glowing from a cluster of buildings in the centre, affording her a better view of the van's path as it weaved around a few small roads and then drove right into the largest of the buildings. With a huge grey roof it looked like an airplane hangar from above, although she could see it was connected to other buildings, linked by what appeared to be corridors. The sound of doors banging closed from below told her this was as far as she would be following in flight. She would need to will her way inside.

Deciding not to attempt to focus on Kyra in case it had the same draining effect as it had before, she concentrated instead on the van. It made no difference though. The electric shock of resistance hit her again, and she knew she wouldn't be able to gain entry to the building. It was useless. Every attempt seemed to be depleting her energy further. There was nothing to do but watch, and wait.

When Crystal appeared suddenly by her side, she was ecstatic; well, as ecstatic as a girl could be with a kidnapped best friend.

"Oh My God, thank goodness you're back. I was on my own. Ray wasn't feeling good. He's gone back to his body but he promises he'll be fine. The van went in there." She pointed below to the doors she'd been watching like an eagle. "What did he say? Liam, I mean."

"Honey, it's not great. He didn't have time to explain, but we need to help him get here and get Kyra out. You did a great job staying with the van. First class. I don't suppose by any chance you remember any of the directions the van took? Even just vaguely?" she asked, and Lauren had something to smile about at last. She reeled off the list of directions and place names she'd memorised to a wide eyed Crystal.

"Wow, way to go! Okay, I'm gonna go tell the guys the directions before I forget them. Don't move an inch," she said and disappeared.

Chapter 59

Kyra awoke gradually, as if something was anchoring her in sleep, unwilling to let her go. Dreams and reality mingled, leaving her confused and incapable of focussing, unable to even open her eyes. Colours and shapes danced, teasing, pretending to form coherent thoughts and images, but then melting and trickling away.

Suddenly, from nowhere, she was assaulted with the memory of a black hood being put roughly over her head. And even in sleep she was aware of her heart racing as she was suffocated by fear and confusion. Yet still, she couldn't pull herself from the cloying sleep in which she was submerged. What had happened? She fished with desperation for driftwood of thought, something to cling on to and keep herself afloat. A memory of her friends sailed by and she grabbed it with all her might.

Blurry but real, the memory was of the car park and Noah, of Marco and his mother, and for an instant she was awash with elation as she recalled their achievements with their tools. But those memories soon dispersed, blown away by the breeze, and she recalled the alarm of being ripped from her Dream Ride and back into her body, of being lifted, carried, and having no control over either her physical or energy bodies. Dazed, she'd understood nothing, but had known with certainty she was in danger. And then the hood.

"No!" she screamed, finally dragging herself from the nightmare laden sleep, nightmares that were her reality. Opening her heavy eyes, she winced at the pain that throbbed in her head, and squinted against the brightness of the room she found herself in. It was a bedroom, she realised as she looked around, moving her head slowly to minimise the pain. But not her own bedroom. *Where the hell am I?* The terror of her dreams had followed her into wakefulness and she was shaking all over, a lump rising in her throat, her heart pounding. She'd been kidnapped? By whom? And why?

Wiggling her toes and fingers, she felt no pain. Lifting her legs one at a time and then her arms, she was relieved to find she wasn't bound, although her limbs felt heavy and awkward. She raised a hand to her head and gently probed all over but found no sign of injury. So why the headache? She wondered if she'd been drugged and felt sick at the thought, but couldn't deny the probability. She could remember nothing after the hood had been placed over her head, so her kidnapper must have done *something* to keep her unconscious. Shoving the thought away she took a slow deep breath and told herself to inspect her surroundings, remember as much as she could for when she was rescued.

From where she was lying, she could see the room was lit with a bright bulb in the centre of a white ceiling encased in a floral yellow shade. The walls were painted cream, adorned with pictures of sailboats and sunsets in pine frames. Slowly raising herself onto her elbows, she could see ahead of her a wardrobe and a dressing table on top of which sat a glass of water. Her mouth felt like it was lined with cotton wool. She was desperate for a drink, but not desperate enough to consider consuming anything left by her kidnaper. Turning her head slowly to the right, she could see a bookshelf full of paperbacks and squinted trying to read some titles; but it hurt her head too much so she gave up. The floor was carpeted in soft beige; the overall effect of the room was clean and comfortable, although slightly clinical. None of these observations did anything to diminish her fear.

Turning her head she noticed the door on the wall behind her, solid grey metal, like something in an institution, maybe a prison. That's when hot tears threatened to cascade, but she bit her lip hard, drawing blood, forcing herself to focus and stay calm. She had no idea what was going on or why she was here, but she knew she *had* to get out of here. She was in no doubt that the door was locked, and even if it wasn't she didn't think she wanted to know what, or who, was on the other side. But still she sat up, swinging her legs over the edge of the bed and sliding to the floor. Standing on shaky limbs she padded slowly across the room, keeping her movements to a minimum to avoid the pounding effect each footstep had on her head.

Tugging at the metal handle, she confirmed the door was indeed locked. It wasn't budging an inch. There was a small square window in the door, but it was covered from the outside so she was unable to see beyond. *At least unable to see with my eyes,* Kyra thought, and with a glimmer of hope she rushed back to the bed and lay down once again on the pale blue quilt. She couldn't walk through the door. But she *could* Dream Ride through it; find out where she was. Go and find her friends and get them to send help.

Breathing deeply she tried to calm herself sufficiently for the Ride. Then she lifted up from her body. At least that's what she told herself to do, but it didn't happen. She tried again, and again, and again, growing more frantic with every try. But it just wasn't happening. She remained in her body as if glued there, and with every attempt she grew weaker, more drained. She recognised the sensation of complete lack of energy, but it took her a few minutes to realise where from. The Shadows. It was exactly how she'd felt when they'd appeared during Dream Rides. Were those shadows something to do with her kidnapping? But that didn't make sense, they were *shadows*. Then again, nothing about this made much sense.

Feeling queasy in her stomach, she called out with her mind, *Nana Anna, I need you*. With a sinking feeling she realised instantly her cry for help hadn't travelled beyond the four walls that contained her. She didn't know why or how, but this place had removed all of her abilities. She was on her own.

It was at this precise moment, as she was battling between submitting to the fear and collapsing in a sobbing pile on the bed and devising some kind of escape plan from the evil men who surely must have taken her for unimaginable purposes, that she heard a heavy metallic click. The door opened, admitting a smartly dressed young woman, followed closely by a boy who could be no more than ten years old. This threw Kyra completely, and before she could even think about making a run for it the door had closed again. She cursed herself for missing the opportunity.

"Hi, Kyra. How are you feeling?" the woman asked with a bright smile. She looked about thirty years old, and reminded Kyra of her aunt, with the same bobbed brown hair and a similar style of clothing. She looked just like any other normal person. Kyra forced herself to remember this woman had something to do with snatching her from her own bedroom. Kyra clenched her teeth resolutely, deciding to remain silent and give nothing away until she could work out what these people wanted from her.

The woman wasn't fazed by Kyra's lack of response. "Welcome to our school for extraordinarily talented Dream Riders," she said as if Kyra had just walked in of her own free will. "Now I know you're scared and probably completely baffled, and I am truly sorry we had to come and get you like that. But we noticed that your ability was reaching a high level very quickly and you need guidance how to use it before you are manipulated by those around you. I'll explain in more detail later, and I'm sure once you see the work we do here you'll be proud to become a member." The woman paused at last and put an arm loosely around the shoulder of the young boy who'd been watching Kyra with an interested expression, as if she were a new playmate. *Or a new toy.*

"Now why don't you have a drink and some cake and settle yourself in?" She gestured toward the dressing table at a glass of water and a slice of chocolate cake Kyra hadn't noticed before. "And we'll come back in a while once you're feeling yourself and

223

talk you through who we are and what we do here. I'm sure you have a million questions. Once you've heard what we have to say, we can take you back home before your father and brother notice you're gone." The woman affectionately ruffled the boy's hair and motioned him toward the door with a nod of her head.

Before turning to go, he looked at Kyra with big green eyes and said, "I know you're gonna love this place."

Chapter 60

"Have you heard of Phantoms, Noah?" Liam asked eventually. They'd travelled in near silence for the last ten minutes; all three of them opening their mouths only to debate the directions Crystal had given Liam, which in turn Liam had instructed Marco and Noah to memorise. The silence screamed of tension. Two people were determined to find and rescue somebody they cared about deeply, unwilling to fail, and a third person was desperate to pay back the lifesaving actions this group of people had performed tonight, by doing all he could to assist them in saving one of their own.

Noah was practising breathing techniques to help him stay calm. He wanted to be prepared for anything that might happen when they reached their destination. He refused to let fear creep into his veins, closing a curtain over the possibilities of what may have happened or *be* happening to Kyra. Now and again he'd glanced at Liam in the rear-view mirror, tempted to suggest making a plan, but Liam's gaze had remained fixed on the road ahead. His expression had invited no conversation. The sound of his sudden question startled Noah and also sent waves of anxiety through him.

"Yes, I have actually. I don't know much, but I do know a forum I was on closed down and disappeared as soon as I asked about them. The group has them a couple of times during Dream Rides. Is that what this is all about? Have they got something to do with this – with Kyra?"

"The forums are where they track them, Noah. It's where they seek the Switchers. I stopped using those sites years ago. It's the Phantoms themselves who *run* the majority of those forums. If you try and set one up independently, they soon find out about it and take control. And if you talk about them too much on the forum, they shut it down."

"But, why?" Marco asked from the passenger seat where he'd been following the conversation with interest.

Although there were many more pressing questions, Noah was pleased Marco had lost the sarcastic edge to his voice. He seemed to have finally accepted the Dream Riders, and the situation, as reality.

As usual, Liam didn't answer his question directly. "They're big, Marco. Bigger than you could imagine."

"Left here," Marco called, and Liam made a quick turn onto a narrow lane lined with trees, silvery leaves shimmying in the headlights on both sides of the road.

"What are they? Who are they?" Noah asked, hoping to understand more about these Phantoms, anything, so he might formulate some kind of plan and be in a better position to help Kyra when they arrived. He should have known Liam's answer would be anything but simple.

"They're the opposite of everything Dream Riders believe in. They're the smoke that rises from a burning village. If we don't find Kyra right now, it will be too late."

Hell, there are some things that are impossible to prepare for, Noah realised, letting Liam's words sink in. Maybe Liam made more sense than they gave him credit for.

"Why do they want Kyra?" Marco asked.

"Because she's a Switcher with a very successful future," Liam said, turning for an instant to meet Noah's gaze. Liam's eyes revealed no fear. That should have reassured Noah, given Liam's ability to see the future, but it didn't. As he pictured Kyra's face, her smile, he felt something break inside as he imagined the possibility of losing his best friend.

Chapter 61

Kyra tried the door a few seconds after the woman and child had left, and it was still locked, just as she'd expected it to be. She tried dream riding again too, but it was no good. She considered just going along with them, pretending she was happy and willing to join their team, or club, or whatever they called it, until she was presented with an opportunity to escape. But what if it was too late by then? What would they do to her in the meantime? What did they want from her?

The message was clear, despite their claims: *you are not leaving.* She didn't believe a word that had slipped from the woman's mouth and was under no illusion that they would just let her go home after kidnapping and probably drugging her. Kyra was convinced they would use her for whatever it was they wanted, and then discard her. She shuddered.

Maybe her friends would be looking for her, she thought hopefully. But then she realised if they were they would have Dream Ridden to her by now. And if *her* powers didn't work here, then the likelihood was that neither would theirs. Having been unconscious for the entire journey, she had no idea how far they'd travelled, but she was sure her friends wouldn't be able to find her without being able to connect to her thought energy, regardless of how close to or far away from home she was.

Sitting on the edge of the bed, she rested her head in her hands and let the tears flow at last, the barrier of self-control and confidence breaking and crashing down like an invaded fortress. She was completely out of ideas, stumped. The woman's face swam in her mind again, her blue eyes cold and glaring in defiance of her soft features and her warm smile. Those eyes told Kyra far more than the woman's false words which had attempted to invite Kyra in, enticing her to join this, this *place*. The woman's eyes couldn't lie however hard she tried. Her eyes had told the truth, warning Kyra away, and striking a spark of fear deep inside her, fear that was now feeding on itself and burning into a raging furnace in the pit of her stomach, turning her into a quivering wreck.

At that moment Kyra realised how unaccustomed to fear she was. Not that she considered herself to be brave. She'd just never had cause to experience real terror before. And being a practical person she'd imagined she would have remained calm and strong and continued to seek a solution to her predicament regardless of how helpless it seemed. But right now she was completely blinded by her fear, unable to search for a solution. Paralysed, she was convinced she'd be incapable of action even if the opportunity to escape arose. Like a rabbit caught in a trap, she waited for her hunters to collect her, helpless to do anything about it.

What am I so scared of? She asked herself, attempting to regain control of her emotions. Unlike most people's fears, hers weren't rooted in the uncertainty of death, as she knew life continued on the other side. Although she did fear what they might do to her while she was still alive. She realised her main fear, however, was of them snatching away the opportunity to live her life. Just when everything was good at last, when she'd found friends she *fit* with, when she'd finally begun to feel like she made *sense*, and to look forward to her future, it would all be over, just like that. So much for the big dream riding adventure. It had been less than a week and it was finished.

And then there was Golden Boy. She had no idea who he was or where he came from, but she'd been certain deep inside that they were connected, that they would see each other again and be together in the physical world one day. Fantasies had filled her head day and night of him, of *them*. She'd dreamed of his golden curls, his piercing blue eyes, and she'd been astounded by the strength of her own emotions, the way her whole body sparkled at just the thought of him, the way she felt *complete* when she simply looked at him. She was consumed by him and had spent every waking moment anticipating the next time she'd see him. Now it seemed she'd been wrong. It wasn't the beginning of great inter-dimensional love affair destined to span this lifetime and many others. She was nothing more than a silly girl caught up in a teenage crush, just like those she'd made fun of so often.

At that moment, just when she'd reached the very depths of despair, something changed both inside and outside of her. Suddenly her energy soared and all fear and sadness was stripped away from her like a heavy drape being drawn back. In that instant she was filled with golden light and at the same time the whole room was illuminated with the same magnificent glow. She knew it was Golden Boy before she'd even raised her head and she wondered how she ever could have doubted him. When she raised her head her cheeks were red and tear stained; her eyes puffy and moist. He smiled and his eyes shone even brighter than the rest of him. His golden hair was tousled around his head, soft and curly. His features were as perfect as she remembered them.

"You came," she whispered.

"I will always come," he replied, his words singing out in a beautiful accent.

"Who are you? Why are you here?" she asked. Determined to learn something about him, all fear evaporated. It didn't matter to her where she was at this moment in time. All that mattered was that he was here, and she knew as long as he was here everything would be okay.

"My name is Anjo. I am here to return you to safety, Kyra. It's very important that you survive," he said softly, and moved toward the door.

"But why? Why do you care? You don't know me," she replied, and he fixed his gaze on hers.

"Yes I do, Kyra. I know you better than you understand. Your survival is vital for many people in this world." His gaze was so intense she thought her heart would stop.

"Especially for me," he added. She had so many questions, but she was speechless.

"You must leave this place now," Anjo said, and she smiled.

"Well, yeah, I was kinda thinking the same thing but... " Before she could finish the sentence, he'd disappeared and she heard the very definite click of the lock. *He's opened the door,* she realised, shocked. Without stopping to think or worry about where he'd gone, she sprung into action and leapt from the bed, filled again with the determination she thought she'd lost and a very strong will to survive. She was glowing, far happier than a girl should be in her current situation. *He came to save me. He really came to save me.*

Pulling the door open just a crack, she peered out carefully to see what lay beyond. It appeared to be a dim white corridor leading both ways, and she was relieved to see there was nobody within her line of sight. Easing the door open farther, she fought the urge to just run and leaned forward until her whole head was out the door. Looking around quickly, she could see that in both directions the corridor disappeared around a corner around fifty metres away. There was nothing to distinguish between the two options, no flashing EXIT sign; and she remained static, unable to make a decision in case she made the wrong one and ran right into the arms of her captors.

Then suddenly, from nowhere, she just knew with complete clarity that she needed to go left. She didn't even stop to question it, and pulling the door quietly closed behind her she began hurriedly but quietly walking in that direction. Sure enough when she looked up she could see a golden glow emanating from around the corner. She smiled.

Chapter 62

They'd finally reached the destination and Liam had confirmed with Crystal that they were in the right place. But there was a problem. A high metal fence bordered the perimeter of the site and it was topped with very nasty looking loops of barbed wire. There was no way anybody could scale it in their physical body without being ripped to shreds. And right now it was a physical body Kyra needed to help her get out of there. The gates were locked tight too.

"Maybe it's time to call the police now?" Noah asked as Liam rattled the gates again, trying to force them open. Marco paced farther along the fence, inspecting every inch on the off chance there might be a gap or hole.

"And what would we tell them? That we followed the directions of invisible people who pursued a van that they imagined *might* be carrying my sister? Oh, and we could add that Marco stole his dad's car to get here. By the time we'd even convinced them we were serious, *anything* could have happened to her." He was scraping at the ground with a large stick as he talked, probing to see if there was any chance of digging a hole underneath, but getting nowhere fast. Marco had disappeared around the corner of the fence.

"What do they want from her?" he asked, not sure he wanted to know the answer.

"They want her power. I'm not too sure why, but people like her have something special that Phantoms can't replicate. So they'll either try to convince her, or force her to help them in order to feed their greed." He paused from his digging and looked up at Noah. "Hey that rhymed – feed and greed."

Noah looked at him incredulously, failing to find any humour in the situation. He glanced around nervously, growing more fearful every minute. The sky had begun to clear now, and the early morning moon cast an eerie blue glow on everything it touched.

"What do you mean replicate?"

"Well, I don't think Phantoms Dream Ride naturally, not in the same way you and I Dream Ride. Well, not the same way *I* Dream Ride. They travel on a different vibration, darker, denser, which is why they appear like shadows, because they're essentially in a different place. This means they can only *watch* us Dream Riding. They can't interfere. They do it for observational purposes, to assess prospective targets."

"So they chose Kyra because of what she did – on the car park?" he asked, and a movement from the corner of his eye made him jump. But it was only Marco walking toward them.

"Yes, very probably. Kyra is an extremely skilled Dream Rider." He was breathing heavily now with the effort of digging.

"But she's okay right now? I mean, she's not been harmed?"

"Your friends haven't been able to see her yet. They can't get in to the building, Noah, just like they couldn't get into the van. These Phantoms weaken your energy whenever you're near them. I don't know why. I guess they must have purposefully increased that effect around their buildings and vehicles."

"Oh God, we have to get in there," he said, alarmed. This was taking too long. Anything could have happened to her.

Liam stopped what he was doing and looked up at Noah. "Do you think I'm trying to dig a hole in the ground just for fun?" he asked. "It's no bloody good; this fence goes way under the ground." He stood.

Just then Noah noticed something glowing to the right of the gate. He pointed toward the fence, speechless, and Liam turned to look just as the glow faded. A hole had appeared in the fence, about two metres in diameter, the edges of it were still glowing with a yellow light.

"How... " Noah started.

"I don't care how. Let's get in there," Liam said, stepping through the hole. Noah followed, motioning to Marco who was now only a few feet away.

Once inside the perimeter, Liam paused, closing his eyes and the other boys watched him expectantly. When he opened his eyes again a few seconds later he said, "Ray's back now and feeling fine. This way."

He jogged toward some buildings to the left and the others followed. They passed several small buildings and a lot of parked cars and then turned right and passed through a shadowy alleyway between two brick buildings. When they emerged they could see before them a vast structure as large as an airplane hangar.

"She's in here somewhere. These are the doors the van drove into."

Two huge doors faced them, and using the shadows of parked cars as cover, they made their way toward them. It didn't take a genius to figure out they'd be locked, but they tried them anyway. The entire time Noah glanced anxiously into every shadow despite the fact that Marco had picked up a large stick and assigned himself the position of guard. Definitely locked, Liam confirmed, and surveyed the area, looking up and down the wall for another way in, a window, another door. Tapping Noah on the shoulder, Marco pointed at something to their right and opened his mouth as if to speak, but no words emerged. Noah and Liam followed the direction of his pointed finger with their eyes.

It was a light, an intense golden light hovering about ten feet above the ground. To Noah it seemed like a sparkling star that had been captured and pulled toward the Earth. It was stunning, completely breathtaking, emitting not only a luminous glow but also a sense of peace and calm. Then suddenly it moved, floating as if it had a mind of its own, and it drifted away from them and around the corner of the building.

"What was that?" Noah asked.

But Liam didn't answer; he simply ran after the light. And Noah was shocked to actually hear him laughing. Looking at Marco, he raised his eyebrows.

Marco shrugged his shoulders. "Mate, this just keeps getting weirder."

They ran after Liam and as they rounded the corner the light was visible up ahead, hovering about twenty metres in front of them. It was directly above a metal door, and as the three of them walked closer the light flittered downward and seemed to actually disappear into the door, merging with the metal until the whole thing appeared to be charged with light. In the deepness of the night's silence, the loud click of the door unlocking was deafening. Noah braced himself, expecting a furious security guard to come bursting through.

But Liam turned the handle, evidently fearless, and pulled the door open, whispering, "Thank you, thank you so much."

Chapter 63

Kyra rounded the corner of the corridor and stopped dead in her tracks. Maybe she'd been wrong about the feeling. Maybe she'd taken the wrong direction; because dead ahead of her, she could see a door opening. Heart thudding, she realised she didn't have time to turn back before she was seen. As the door opened fully she could see three figures silhouetted against the gloomy light of the night beyond.

There is nothing to be scared of she thought, and realised the fear was of her own making. Anjo wouldn't have directed her toward danger. She just knew it. In her gut she was sure the figures ahead of her were no threat. Just then she heard footsteps coming from behind her, around the corner, and then a shout, "She's gone! The Sutton girl's gone!" And then there were more footsteps, running now, running toward her.

Putting all her faith into Anjo and her own instinct, she ran forward as fast as her tired legs would carry her, not daring to look behind. She zoomed through the door shouting, "They're behind me; they're coming. *Come on,*" to the three figures she now registered to be her brother, Marco, and Noah. She had no time to feel relieved to see them and didn't stop running until she was a good distance from the door, when she turned and realised only Noah and Marco had followed her.

"Liam, come on," she called again, terrified, as a man and woman emerged from the door behind him. Hearing a noise in the other direction, she spun around quickly to see two burly men stepping out from behind a van just a few metres ahead of her. She backed away slowly. Noah and Marco followed suit.

"Whatever happens," she whispered, "I'm glad I got to see you again, Noah. Thank you for coming to rescue me." She glanced to her left, and Noah smiled weakly. Then turning to her right she said, "And thank you too, Marco. I don't know how or why you're here, but thank you."

"I owed you," he replied.

Chapter 64

The rollercoaster of emotions he'd experienced throughout this phenomenal night was enough to give him a heart attack. He was a wreck. Now his relief at seeing Kyra in one piece and seemingly uninjured had been quickly dwarfed by the dread that drenched him when he realised they were trapped. The two men ahead of them looked extremely unfriendly and impossibly *huge*. The men started toward them, closing in, and the three of them backed away faster still.

They reached Liam and turned again, to see the man and woman who'd just come through the door blocking their escape in that direction. More loud voices floated from within the building. Noah considered making a break to the side, but was in no doubt the colossal men would catch him and probably flatten him with a little finger. "What now, Liam?" he whispered.

"Let's just see what happens," Liam said, sounding surprisingly calm considering their predicament.

"Well you can see the future can't you?"

"Yeah, I can, and it looks pretty bright."

Directly above them the light that had directed them, their guiding star, appeared once again. They all looked up in awe and Noah gasped as the small twinkling torch suddenly expanded and grew into a powerful beacon, radiant, engulfing the night sky. In the small area where they stood it seemed like daylight had arrived and no one could take their eyes from the spectacular sight.

Chapter 65

As Anjo appeared above her, his light a dazzling luminescence radiating all around, Kyra knew she was safe. She could hear the gasps of her friends. "Can you see him?" she asked.

"Him? I can see a light, a really bright light." Noah replied, turning his head from the brilliance. Anjo was smiling at her, as he hovered above, and his smile made her forget everything.

"Kyra, only you can see me. Only you can view this dimension while you're still in your body. Others can see my light when I want them to, but that's all. They don't see *me*," he explained. She tore her eyes away from him and looked at the people around her.

The Nasties (as she'd come to think of her kidnappers) had raised their hands as if in self-defence and were backing away. Noah and Marco had also shielded their faces against the blinding brightness of the light and Liam, behind her, was just squinting and grinning like a lunatic. Suddenly the man and woman turned and ran inside, slamming the door firmly behind them; and after a couple more tentative backward steps, the two ugly goons also turned and fled into the night, or possibly back to the cave they'd crawled out of.

"What? Where did they go?" Marco asked, perplexed. Kyra didn't know the answer, but she knew it had something to do with Anjo, who'd dimmed his radiance and descended to ground level. He moved toward her.

"Kyra has a Protector. Even Phantoms won't mess with Protectors. I'd say that's the last we'll see of them," Liam explained. "You're a pretty big deal, little sis," he smiled at her.

"Is it true?" she asked, turning back toward Anjo. "What does he mean?"

"It's true, Kyra. I came here to keep you safe from harm so you can accomplish your goals in this life." He was now standing in front of her, looking for all inents and purposes like a normal Dream Rider. Well, a kind of *glowing* and seriously *gorgeous* Dream Rider.

"Who's she talking to?" Kyra heard Marco whisper in the background, but she ignored him.

"So you're, like, a real person too, right?" she asked.

He laughed at that, his eyes crinkling at the corners and her heart flipped. He suddenly appeared even less translucent, almost solid, as he answered, "Yes, Kyra, I am real. Like you, it took me a long time to wake up to what I am, to my reality. And then it took longer still to learn all I could do, to re-discover my mission here, and to find you."

"Wow." She wondered something else then. "So you only visited me because I'm your... mission... "

"Maybe I chose my words wrongly. You're not just my mission, Kyra. You're my purpose."

I was right. I was so right.

"Will we ever meet for real?" The question escaped in a whisper.

"Anything is possible, Kyra. But I must go now."

"Thank you, Anjo. For saving me." There was so much more she wanted to say but she knew it wasn't the time.

"*Adeus.* I will visit soon, I promise," he said as he vanished into the night sky, which had now lightened from deepest black to a dark purple.

Kyra puzzled at the unfamiliar language, and making a mental note to look it up she felt a little buzz that she might discover something more about Anjo. She turned to her brother and her friends who were watching her patiently.

"Well that was an interesting conversation. The side we heard, anyway. Do we get to hear the answers to your questions?" Liam asked.

"Of course," she smiled. "We all have a lot to explain, I guess. But wait, we shouldn't talk about it without the others, the group's not complete. Let's wait until we're all together."

"Oh they're here, Ky. You don't think we managed to get here all on our own do you?" Noah asked as Liam put an arm around her shoulder and began steering her toward the gate.

Of course they're here she thought and looked up toward the sky. "Thank you guys, thank you all. You are the best friends ever."

Chapter 66

"So you really don't think they'll come after me again?" Kyra asked, taking another sip of her orange juice.

"I really honestly don't think they will, Ky," Noah replied patiently. It was about the tenth time he'd reassured her. They were sitting around the dining table in the DiCarmello house with Marco and Lauren, waiting for the others to arrive. "Liam said they're still out there and they might be watching you, but they're highly unlikely to do anything. They'll probably move on to other targets. You're fully protected. I've done some research, which I might add is a lot more difficult now that I know I have to try and be covert on the forums and stay under their radar. But anyway, Protectors don't come from the Spirit World, not the same place as Nana Anna, anyway. They come from a different dimension. It's known as the "Light World.""

"Wow! That sounds pretty intense. I'd love to visit it sometime," Lauren said as she checked her make-up in a small hand held mirror.

"Well I don't think that's going to happen any time in the near future. It's a pretty advanced dimension. They don't just let anyone in," Noah smiled.

"Why me?" Kyra asked. "Do all dream riders have Protectors?"

He shook his head and said, "Only very few, those who are destined to change the course of humanity."

"I'm going to change the course of humanity?" she asked, incredulous, and even Lauren looked up from her phone and whistled, impressed.

"It would appear so."

"See Ky? I always told you that you were odd for a reason," Lauren winked. "Just don't forget us lowly people when you're rich and famous."

"If I make it onto Oprah one day, you'll all be right there with me," Kyra joked and took a deep breath, filing the astonishing information away to take out and examine in more detail later.

"I still don't get why those blokes legged it like a bunch of chicken shaped girls when that light guy showed up," Marco said.

"Well, I think Protectors possess a very high level of energy. You could even call it a power. I think this Phantom organisation knows very well that Protectors even have the ability to influence physical matter in the most complex ways in order to protect their charge," Noah said, and then stood from his chair and paced the room again. He'd been up and down like a yoyo since they'd arrived at Marco's house.

"Noah, what is wrong with you?" Kyra asked. "You're making me nervous."

"It's just that I've never skipped school before. What if we get in trouble?" He looked at her with fear in his eyes and she laughed as she realised he looked more scared now than he had when attempting to rescue her from her evil kidnappers.

"It's not funny!" he protested.

"Look mate," Marco said. "I'm famous for writing top quality parent's letters. So don't worry, you won't get busted. You can just think of it as my tool." A smile spread across his face.

"Yeah, but this doesn't even look anything like my mum's signature," Noah complained taking out the forged letter and examining it again.

"Give it a rest, will ya? They're not gonna check it against the records. You're teacher's pet. Anyway, I'm sure you'll get used to it."

"Oh no, not me. This is the first and last time. And I'm only skipping today because of extraordinary circumstances," he said crossing his arms.

"Extraordinary situations require extraordinary measures. It can be useful sometimes, a day off here and there, you know," Marco said.

"Look Marco, I think you should be thinking less about skipping school and more about how you're going to do what your mum asked you to," Kyra suggested.

"I know, I know. I've been thinking about it. You lot did say you'd help me, didn't you?" he asked sheepishly. Kyra realised he wasn't used to asking for help. It wasn't an easy thing for him to do.

"Of course we will. Don't forget, nice and subtle. It will take time," she advised.

The doorbell rang then and Lauren hopped up excitedly as Noah disappeared into the hallway, and returned a few seconds later with Liam, Crystal, and Ray in tow.

"Who's for curry?" Liam said holding up two white carrier bags.

"Yummy," Kyra said, her tummy rumbling in appreciation. It was hungry business all this dream riding.

"Fantastic, everyone's here. We can have our debriefing meeting while we eat," Lauren exclaimed reaching out for Ray's hand. Kyra rolled her eyes. "Oh, and Noah, we need to make a plan for your Dream Riding lessons too."

Noah smiled. "Don't worry Lauren. What's meant to be will be."

With Crystal's help Marco began opening the foil containers and dishing out rice and curry onto plates. Kyra watched him with a smile. The house seemed a lot brighter than last time she'd been in it, and so did Marco for that matter. It was amazing how much difference some positive energy could make.

"Hey, girls. I'm booking you in for clothes shopping on Saturday. Only a week 'til the Beckridge Centre!" Lauren said, "We are going to have the *best* time."

"Sounds fun," Crystal said. "I haven't actually had a chance to try out the shops here yet."

"But why can't I just wear something I've already got... " Kyra began but stopped when she saw Lauren's warning glare.

There was the sound of a key turning in the front door then, and Kyra noticed Marco freeze, his hand holding a spoonful of Chicken Korma, poised in mid air. Crystal looked at him and smiled. "It'll be fine, don't worry," she said quietly, placing a hand on his arm.

Mr. DiCarmello walked into the kitchen and stopped when he noticed them all, his eyes wide. Kyra realised it must have been the first time his son had brought friends home in years. He glanced around, and muttered, "Err, hello."

"Dad, meet my friends," Marco said, and bit his lip nervously.

"Hi, everyone. It's nice to meet you," he said politely but awkwardly, still looking dumbfounded.

"Well I must say it's very nice to meet you too Mr. D.," Liam said stepping forward and shaking the man's hand enthusiastically. The rest of the group said a cheerful "hello" as if nothing was out of the ordinary.

"Fancy some dinner, dad?" Marco asked. "I promise it's not burnt."

Chapter 67

Later that evening, Kyra fell into bed after a long soak in the bath tub. Physically, she felt tip-top, although she knew she should probably be exhausted, but mentally she was burned out. There was so much to think about and puzzle over, but right now she wanted nothing more than to empty her mind and relax. Leaning back against the headboard she closed her eyes and sighed.

"Hello, Pickle," said Nana Anna. Kyra opened her eyes in surprise.

"Hi, Nana. Where's Elvis? There is no Elvis!" She had *never* seen Nana Anna without her musical accompaniment.

"Oh, I got bored of him. Time for a change. Talking of which, do you like my new rags?" she asked, standing up and twirling around to show off a smart beige trouser suit.

"Wow. You look amazing!" Kyra said. And she meant it. "But what's all this change in aid of?"

"We've both reached a new milestone on our paths, Buttercup. You've done a good job, Kyra, and I have too. But there's nothing more I can teach you, and yet so much more you have to learn."

"But I'll always need your help, Nana Anna," Kyra argued.

"No, you don't need me, my love. And I have other things I need to do too, other places to go."

"But I don't want you to go," Kyra, distraught, couldn't help the tears flowing down her cheeks. Why did it feel like Nana Anna was saying goodbye?

"It doesn't mean you can't visit me, Blossom. It's about time you popped over to my place." She smiled. "It will never be goodbye, only ever see you later."

"Nana Anna," Kyra called, but the old lady had gone already.

Kyra slipped into her energy body and called again to her Nana, but nothing. She tried to sense her, to locate her, so she could follow, but again, nothing. *What does she mean I can go and see her? How can I do that when I can't even follow her?* Kyra wondered, distressed.

Suddenly, the night sky outside her window was illuminated with gold. The glow spread into her room and then reached right inside her, casting a beam of light on the dark shadows of her sadness. She turned to see Anjo outside, waiting for her.

THE END

Your Gifts

We might not all be able to fly or time travel like the Dream Riders, but we did all come here with our own unique gifts to share with the world. What are your special gifts? You can usually figure it out by thinking about what you love to do - it could be drawing, writing, cooking, singing, dancing, making people laugh... there's an endless list! When you share your gifts with the world you are really fulfilling your own mission here on Earth and helping to make the world a better place! Use this space to explore your gifts and what you love to do.

About the Author

Lynda Louise Mangoro lives in Sussex, UK, with her husband, Michael, and their three sons, Samuel, Jacob and Oliver.

Lynda is passionate about learning and discovering spiritual teachings from international cultures, and understanding the threads of underlying and unifying spiritual truths that weave through them. Lynda writes as an expression of her own journey of self discovery.

As well as bringing the Dream Riders to life, Lynda paints portraits and other commissioned artwork, writes and illustrates children's books and offers website and graphic design services.

Visit her website at www.LyndaMangoro.com and follow her on Facebook at www.facebook.com/LyndaMangoroCreations. Lynda can be contacted at lynda@mangoro.co.uk.

Coming Soon

Journey
of the
DREAM RIDERS

A whole new world
awakens...

Join the Dream Riders on their next gripping adventure as they learn more about themselves and the reality of our world, and strive to use their gifts to protect and help others. Can they cast their light on the dark shadows of life – pain, greed, and murder – without sacrificing their own lives?

www.JuicyLivingPublishing.com

Where's the Magic Wand?
by Lynda Mangoro

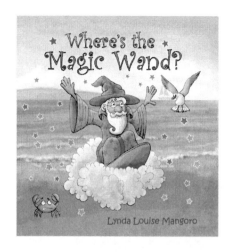

The Wizard has searched high and low for his magic wand but he needs some help. Does anyone believe in magic? Will anyone help him look? Maybe the wizard will tell them the magic secret...

As well as being a memorable and whimsical rhyming story, rich with vibrant illustrations, this tale conveys an important and powerful message – that we all create our realities and shape our lives through our thoughts and beliefs.

Many 'grown-ups' have discovered the truth of this and are beginning to apply it consciously to their own lives, but why not sow the seed of this knowledge at a young age and enable our children to grow up with permission to create the lives they deserve and the understanding that they can achieve anything they put their minds to.

Where's the Magic Wand is the first in the Little Tommy Wonders series, empowering stories for little boys and girls with big questions. Encouraging an inquisitive mind and an open heart...

"Lynda's message is a gift to our children and the world, nurturing their inherent genius and empowering them to shine!"
- Laura Duksta, Ambassador of Love, Author, *You Are a Gift to the World* and New York Times bestseller, *I Love You More*
Www.LauraDuksta.com

 *Juicy Living* Publishing

Juicy Living Publishing was founded by Lilou Macé in 2009 when she published her first book, *I Lost My Job and I Liked It*. In 2011, Lilou went on to launch her Juicy Living Tour, traveling around the world interviewing juicy people, including many renowned authors and teachers, bringing information and inspiration to millions via her Web TV channel. Following her inner guidance system, in early 2011 Lilou was inspired to open her publishing company up to other authors, with the intention of contributing to the global conversation of empowerment and awakening consciousness.

With the inevitable expansion of thoughts and practices that relate to spiritual ideals and internal development during this recognized time of shifting energies, Juicy Living Publishing aims to give authors the opportunity to share their messages and teachings with as wide an audience as possible. Our vision is to produce resources that promote a juicy way of living for all our readers. Worldwide.

Juicy Living Publishing is committed to producing books of high quality and high value to its readers of all ages; children, teens, and adults. We welcome submissions from both published and new authors. Please see our submissions page for guideline at www. JuicyLivingPublishing.com.

Also from Juicy Living Publishing

I LOST MY JOB AND I LIKED IT BY LILOU MACE

Lilou has lost her job. The time has come to test her beliefs to the limit: at a time of global crisis can she use the Law of Attraction to find her dream job, and thereby 'empower millions' to do likewise? This is her 30-day stream-of-consciousness diary, from the moment she was lost her job. Travel with her as she grapples with doubt, relishes avocados and finds something to be grateful for in each and every step of her job search.
ISBN: 978-0-9562546-0-3

I HAD NO MONEY AND I LIKED IT BY LILOU MACE

Lilou Mace's I Had No Money and I Liked It is a wonderful, exciting, fascinating exploration of the power of faith and synchronicity. Written in the form of a journal, we follow Lilou day to day as she faces the challenges of living in the flow of synchronicity, giving herself to what feels authentic and vital to her life. We see her moments of doubt, we feel her uncertainties, and we witness her growing faith in what she is doing. As her faith grows, the world opens up to her in a way that is miraculous.
ISBN: 978-0-9562546-6-5

WHERE'S THE MAGIC WAND? BY LYNDA MANGORO

As well as being a memorable and whimsical rhyming story, rich with vibrant illustrations, this tale conveys an important and powerful message for young children – that we all create our realities and shape our lives through our thoughts and beliefs. What better gift to give them than this powerful knowledge?
ISBN 978-0-9562546-1-0

Lightning Source UK Ltd.
Milton Keynes UK
UKOW052248311011

181250UK00002B/9/P